THE BARCLAYS GUIDE TO

Franchising

for the Small Business

Barclays Small Business Series

Series Editors: Colin Gray and John Stanworth

This new series of highly practical books aimed at new and established small businesses has been written by carefully selected authors in conjunction with the Small Business Unit of Barclays Bank. All the authors have a wide experience of the theory and, more important, the *practice* of small business, and they address the problems that are likely to be encountered by new businesses in a clear and accessible way, including examples and case studies drawn from real business situations.

These comprehensive but compact guides will help owners and managers of small businesses to acquire the skills that are essential if they are to operate successfully in times of rapid change in the business environment.

The Barclays Guide to Marketing for the Small Business
Len Rogers

The Barclays Guide to Computing for the Small Business
Khalid Aziz

The Barclays Guide to International Trade for the Small Business
John Wilson

The Barclays Guide to Financial Management for the Small Business
Peter Wilson

The Barclays Guide to Managing Staff for the Small Business
Iain Maitland

The Barclays Guide to Managing Growth in the Small Business
Colin Gray

The Barclays Guide to Franchising for the Small Business
John Stanworth and Brian Smith

The Barclays Guide to Law for the Small Business
Stephen Lloyd

The Barclays Guide to Buying and Selling for the Small Business
John Gammon

THE BARCLAYS GUIDE TO

Franchising
for the Small Business

JOHN STANWORTH
AND BRIAN SMITH

BARCLAYS
Published by
BLACKWELL

Copyright © John Stanworth and Brian Smith 1991

First published 1991

Basil Blackwell Ltd
108 Cowley Road, Oxford, OX4 1JF, UK

Basil Blackwell, Inc.
3 Cambridge Center
Cambridge, Massachusetts 02142, USA

British Library Cataloguing in Publication Data

A CIP catalogue record for this book is available from the British Library

Library of Congress Cataloging in Publication Data

Stanworth, John
The Barclays guide to franchising for the small business / John Stanworth and Brian Smith.
p. cm. – (Barclays small business series)
ISBN 0–631–17498–2
1. Franchises (Retail trade) I. Smith, Brian. II. Title.
III. Series.
HF5429.23.S73 1991
658.8′708–dc20   90–42898 CIP

Typeset in 10½ on 12½pt Plantin
by Hope Services (Abingdon) Ltd

Contents

Contents

The views contained in this book are not necessarily those of the Bank or its Management. Licence has been given to the authors to research and subsequently to comment as they wish, bearing in mind their high professionalism and considerable experience.

The author and publishers would like to point out that the use of the pronoun 'he' is not gender specific.

Foreword

The last five years have seen a significant growth in the number of small businesses in all sectors of industry in the UK. Unfortunately they have also seen an increase in the numbers of problems encountered by those businesses. Often the problems could have been avoided with the right help and advice.

Barclays, in association with Basil Blackwell, is producing this series of guides to give that help and advice. They are comprehensive and written in a straightforward way. Each one has been written by a specialist in the field, in conjunction with Barclays Bank, and drawing on our joint expertise to ensure that the advice given is appropriate.

With the aid of these guides the businessman or woman will be better prepared to face the many challenges ahead, and, hopefully, will be better rewarded for their efforts.

George Cracknell
Director UK Business Sector
Barclays Bank plc

I

Introduction to franchising

Outline

This chapter looks at:

- the structure of the rest of the book
- the history of franchising
- the British Franchise Association
- different types of franchising
- the future of franchising in the 1990s

In recent years franchising in the United Kingdom has gone through a period of rapid growth. The development of franchising, as a means for conducting business, and its predicted future expansion, should not come as a surprise. Franchising is a system of distribution which, when carried on in an ethical manner, brings identifiable benefits to franchisees and franchisors as well as to the consumers of the goods or services offered.

This book has been written to provide advice both to businesses which may be considering franchising as a means of expansion and to those rather larger numbers who are looking at taking up a franchise as an entry to business. It should also be of use to professional advisers in the franchising field.

In this chapter we examine the history of franchising, describe its development and examine its future prospects. In addition, we will look at a definition of franchising and discuss its various forms.

Later chapters guide the reader through the vast range of business activities that may be franchised, from hamburgers to computers, and outline the comparative strengths and weaknesses of franchising from the viewpoint of all parties. For those wishing to become a franchisee, chapter 4 defines the steps and considerations involved and includes tips on how to select the correct franchise for each individual. Chapter 5 sets out the processes involved in setting up as a franchisor, from market testing through to the final business product. The relationship between the franchisor and franchisee will be formally encapsulated in an agreement. Chapter 6 examines the relationship and includes not only tips but also the possible pitfalls to be avoided.

In chapter 7 we present a franchise checklist questionnaire which can be completed by the reader. In chapter 8 we bring together our overview and conclusions. Finally, in chapter 9, we have included useful addresses and sources of information for those who wish to take their interest further.

Many would suggest that franchising is a recent phenomenon, perhaps one that dates back to the 1950s. However, in its more basic forms its roots can be traced as far back as the Middle Ages.

> All franchises and liberties of the bisshoppericks . . . deryvid from the crowne 1559.

> Fairs, Markets and other franchises c. 1630.
> *Oxford English Dictionary*, 1933

Barons were granted the franchise to collect taxes, in a specified territory, by the King, in return for various services such as the provision of soldiers for an army.

Freemen or citizens of a city were permitted (given the franchise) to sell their wares on city land at markets and fairs in return for payment.

These elements of rights, or freedoms, given to exploit a situation in a specified place in return for a consideration, form the basis of franchising throughout the ages.

The tied house system

Franchising in a more recognizable form can be seen in the British 'tied house' system used by brewers as long ago as the early 1800s. The widespread availability of alcohol was causing social concern. Legislation was introduced to restrict the sale of alcohol to those with licences and also to require innkeepers to improve the drinking environment.

This had two effects: first inns with licences greatly increased in value, making it financially difficult to purchase an inn. In addition, those with licences often had insufficient funds to improve their properties and were therefore likely to go out of business.

The tied house system developed as a defensive mechanism by brewers to retain their selling outlets. In exchange for the grant of a loan or the lease for a property the brewer secured the inn as an exclusive outlet for his beer and spirits. The 'tied' house system proved itself as an efficient business mechanism and still continues today.

US developments

The history of franchising then moves to the United States and to a different form of franchising introduced by the Singer Sewing machine company. At the end of the American Civil War in the mid 1800s, Singer had established a mass manufacturing production system allowing them to sell at a very competitive price. Unfortunately sewing machine servicing and a replacement part service could not be run economically as a central operation. A franchising system was established giving financially independent operators exclusive selling and servicing rights within defined territories. These early franchises were effectively distribution agreements with the added obligation on the franchisee to service the machines upon demand.

Although the Singer scheme had declined before the end of the century, others recognized the use of the franchise system to increase market penetration. In 1898, General Motors used independent businesses to increase their number of distribution outlets without the need for investment. The franchisee (or dealer) was granted an exclusive territory, giving protection against competition from other franchisees and guaranteeing a large volume of sales. However, the dealer could not sell vehicles produced by other manufacturers and was required to inject his own capital into the business to offer the level of service and project the image associated

3

with the franchisor. Motor vehicle dealerships are predominantly franchised to this day.

Soft drink bottlers

General Motors were closely followed by Rexall, who franchised their drug stores. One of the most successful early franchises was the soft drinks bottling industry. Coca-Cola, Pepsi and 7-Up initiated the use of franchising as an economic method of expansion. These products all contain a high water content, which makes production and distribution from one central point financially prohibitive. Through a franchise the companies were able to produce the concentrated drink syrup at a central unit, distribute it to local bottling plants owned and operated by franchisees, who in turn would administer local retail sales. The returnable bottle was also an economic option within local territories. A highly effective franchise was developed and is still used today.

Further developments

The notion of franchising as a business form in the United States moved to wholesaler–retailer relationships in the 1920s. Even at this time the large retailers were seen to be pricing the independent ones out of the market.

The wholesaler (or franchisor) allowed the small retailer (the franchisee) to benefit from large quantity discounts using a common brand name, whilst retaining his independence. In addition, the customer recognized the retailer as offering a known quality product. In later years the business relationship proved additionally beneficial to the retailer in giving him access to prime sites in shopping malls. Without this business alliance, a property developer would consider the small retailer a high risk tenant. In the UK this type of franchise was used by Spar and VG grocery stores.

As a response to economic conditions in the 1930s, oil companies in the United States decided to operate their stations as franchised units. Previously the majority of petrol stations had been company owned, but it was found that many stations became locally uncompetitive in the petrol price war. Through renting the stations to franchisees, the oil companies received rental income and were able to dictate the use of the corporate image while the franchisees were able to set prices according to local conditions. The result was a noticeable increase in petrol sales.

Until the 1950s the majority of companies who operated as franchisors viewed franchising as an efficient method of distribution for products and services which already existed. Car manufacturers, oil companies and soft drink distributors are all examples of the traditional or first generation franchising system.

Franchising boom

The franchising boom of the 1950s is attributed to the second generation franchise which is commonly known as the 'business format franchise'. It recognizes a franchise system as a distinct method of doing business from the outset with the franchisor benefiting from rapid growth with limited risk and the franchisee buying into a proven business system.

Wimpy, the hamburger restaurant chain, was the first business format franchise to set up in the UK. J. Lyons & Co acquired the world-wide franchising rights, outside the USA, from the originator of the concept, Eddie Gold. Wimpy commenced trading in the UK in 1955.

ServiceMaster, the carpet and upholstery cleaning franchise, was another American import which came to the UK in 1958 when Raymond Crouch bought the master licence for Europe from ServiceMaster Industries Inc, a Chicago based company. Mr Softee and Lyons Maid are also credited with offering franchises during the 1950s.

Events in both the UK and United States slowed the growth of franchising in the 1960s. In the UK, the public linked franchising with pyramid selling, a fraudulent marketing scheme. Pyramid selling involves the sale of distributorships to purchasers, who are encouraged with financial incentives to subdivide their distributorship to 'sub-distributors' and so on. The system can be likened to the chain letter principle. At one end of the chain, a door-to-door sales force found the unknown product very difficult to sell, while at the top of the pyramid a fortune had been amassed from the effective sale of multi-level distributorships rather than products.

The government passed legislation in 1973 under the Fair Trading Act, to try and control (but not outlaw) pyramid selling. A legitimate franchisor may inadvertently infringe the Act and should therefore seek legal advice in formulating a franchise agreement. Equally there are some flaws in the legislation and franchisees should also be wary.

The franchise boom in the United States faltered in 1969 when the stock market went into a decline and the economy wavered. Investors considered that their money was safer in a bank than in a business of which they had no prior knowledge.

In the early 1970s there were some attempts in the UK to establish a franchisors' trade association in order to set aside the bad publicity aroused by pyramid selling. Lunches, which were held at the offices of the *Financial Times*, failed to attract Wimpy and Kentucky Fried Chicken whose membership was considered important. However, late in 1977 the British Franchise Association (BFA) was formed with the following organizations as founder members: Budget Rent-a-Car Limited, Dyno-Rod plc, Holiday Inns Inc, Kentucky Fried Chicken Ltd, Prontaprint Limited, ServiceMaster Limited, Wimpy International Limited and Zeibart Mobile Transport Service Limited.

The size and reputation of the founders guaranteed respect for the BFA and franchising in the UK. The BFA has earned all-party support in Parliament and its existence has been instrumental in leading a period of rapid expansion in franchising in the UK. Much of the growth in franchising in the 1980s can be attributed to public trust in BFA members, who are the subject of a strict code of conduct. The address of the BFA can be found in chapter 9. Other reasons for the growing popularity of franchising include the increased importance of service industries which readily lend themselves to franchising, for example, domestic cleaning. In addition, the Government has been keen to encourage self-employment and the growth of small businesses through various initiatives and, finally, banks have become alert to franchising and are able to offer the support of specialists and a range of financial packages.

An insight into the history and development of franchising as a business system are a necessary prerequisite to understanding the basis of franchising. Many attempts have been made to try and arrive at a concise definition of franchising but most tend to omit certain forms or types of franchise.

BFA definition

The BFA has developed its own definition as follows:

> A contractual licence granted by one person (the franchisor) to another (the franchisee) which:
>
> (a) permits or requires the franchisee to carry on, during the period of the franchise, a particular business under or using a specific name belonging to or associated with the franchisor; and
>
> (b) entitles the franchisor to exercise continuing control during the period of the franchise over the manner in which the franchisee carries on the business which is the subject of the franchise; and
>
> (c) obliges the franchisor to provide the franchisee with assistance in carrying on the business which is the subject of the franchise (in relation to the organisation of the franchisee's business, the training of staff, merchandising management or otherwise); and
>
> (d) requires the franchisee periodically during the period of the franchise, to pay the franchisor sums of money in consideration for the franchise, or for goods or services provided by the franchisor to the franchisee; and
>
> (e) which is not a transaction between a holding company and its subsidiary (as defined in section 736 of the Companies Act 1985) or between subsidiaries of the same holding company, or between an individual and a company controlled by him.

A franchise is therefore a contract in which the business terms are expressed. As previously noted both franchisor and franchisee should seek legal advice before compiling or signing a franchise agreement. Misunderstanding of the terms of the contract could have a dramatic effect on the income and future of either party.

Under the contract the franchisee must or is allowed to use the trade name of the franchisor. In many franchises this is the major attraction to the franchisee, who recognizes that the use of a household name, such as McDonald's, will draw custom that he personally could not generate. Similarly, a franchisor would not consider franchising a unique product to a franchisee who was not bound to use it under the franchisor's trade name. This requirement, therefore, protects both parties.

Throughout the period of the franchise, the franchisor retains control of the manner in which the business is run. This is viewed by the franchisor as essential, for a dissatisfied customer at one outlet is unlikely to patronize another. However, a satisfied customer will search out the services or goods again, rather than look to a competitor. By maintaining control over each outlet the franchisor can guarantee the standard of any business bearing his trade mark.

In return the BFA expect the franchisor to assist the franchisee in carrying on his business. The first stage in this process, although not specifically defined, is an initiation programme. Before accepting the franchisee into his business, the franchisor has a duty to assess his suitability.

Once this is established and the contract has been signed, the franchisee has the right to be provided with the necessary training prior to opening. Deficiencies in this process are bound to detract from the uniform quality of the service or goods provided. The support of the franchisor should extend beyond initial training and many franchisors provide specialist advice from a central point as well as regional assistance.

The franchisee is expected to pay the franchisor regularly for the use of the trade name and/or for any goods or services supplied. This is the financial reward to the franchisor in exchange for his trade name, support and goods. The fee may be fixed or calculated as a percentage of gross receipts or, in a few cases, as a percentage of gross profit. The franchisor may also have a mark-up on the goods supplied.

The final paragraph of the BFA definition excludes transactions between companies within a group from the franchise relationship, many of which might otherwise be conceived as being of a franchising nature.

Business format franchise

The BFA definition goes some way to explaining the nature of a business format franchise. However, one area which it does not explore is ownership and capital investment. There are a number of franchises, primarily van sales operations, where an initial investment is not required and the franchisee does not build equity in the business. The system is similar to a tenanted public house. The tenant buys the stock and fixtures and fittings in the pub. On giving up the tenancy these are sold but no consideration is paid for the trade or goodwill.

There tends to be a greater turnover in franchisees in this type of franchise as there are obvious limitations on income and growth potential. If a franchise is to succeed, the franchisee should own the business. If he merely manages the business the franchisee may not have the necessary motivation to guarantee success. The capital sum invested by the franchisee is an additional incentive to do well. Equally, the franchisees should have the right to sell the business in order to reap the rewards of his effort. Accordingly, franchisors will build into the agreement an option to purchase the franchise or to censor the likely purchaser.

The BFA restricts membership of the Association to franchisors who have operated a company-owned pilot scheme for at least a year. This shows that the franchise is workable. It also gives the franchisor the opportunity to reassess his system before offering it to a franchisee.

So far in this chapter, we have looked at the history and essential characteristics of franchising. The range of businesses that may be franchised is discussed in chapter 2, but it may be useful to pause for a moment and examine how franchises can be divided into different subgroups.

Franchise groupings

In the early 1970s many writers considered the following divisions as appropriate:

(i) The manufacturer–retailer franchise: The manufacturer is the franchisor and the retailer, as franchisee, sells the product direct to the public. Examples of this type of franchise would be car dealerships and oil companies.
(ii) The manufacturer–wholesaler franchise: The best example of this franchise is the soft drink companies who license independent bottlers as franchisees.
(iii) The wholesaler–retailer franchise: This might be a co-operative of retailers forming a wholesaling company to act as franchisor and then contractually obliging the retailer to purchase through the co-operative. Alternatively an independent wholesaler may sell his products to a franchisee, such as Spar or VG.
(iv) The trade mark, trade-name, licensor–retailer franchise: The franchisor, not necessarily the manufacturer, may have a service or product which is marketed under a common trade name generally by means of a standard operation. There are many examples of this type of franchise from the fast-food restaurant chain to the domestic service organization.

This early categorization effectively subdivided first generation franchises into three classes, leaving second generation franchises in one class. The remarkable growth of the business format franchise in the last decade has largely rendered this subgrouping system redundant. When subgrouping first-generation franchising, commentators concentrated on the relationship that existed between the franchisor and the franchisee.

Business format franchises have tended to be categorized by the size of the initial investment as follows:

Job franchise	'Where the franchisor is creating a well-paid job for the self-employed man'. 'The largest part of the investment is the purchase price of a van.'
Business franchises	'Much larger investment . . . business premises', 'employs additional staff '.

Investment franchises 'Relatively large investment', 'return on investment the prime exercise'.

The qualifications which writers have found it necessary to use and the unwillingness of franchisors to identify with a specific group indicate the difficulty of this type of classification. There are, as previously mentioned, a handful of franchise systems where the franchisee does not own the business and these, by virtue of this limitation, could be seen as always being in the first category above.

It could be argued that these groups are more a variable of the franchisee and his actions than of the franchise offered.

There are numerous examples of investors buying into the service, van-type operations operating out of business premises and putting several vans on the road. Conversely many 'business franchisees' work, out of necessity, in their retail operation. For McDonald's franchisees this is a prerequisite for newcomers to the business even though the cost of the franchise is in the region of £400,000.

Future growth

The future growth of franchising will depend upon its increased acceptance as a business form. If we re-examine the start of franchising in the UK, it is evident that initially the franchise system was used to market a unique idea. Wimpy distributed, through a franchise operation, the first American hamburger and with it came the notion of fast food with a limited menu. Franchisees found the Wimpy franchise attractive, they were a unique provider of fast food and Wimpy gained maximum geographical coverage at a level of minimum investment.

ServiceMaster Limited, another early franchisor within the UK, also had an original idea to market. Until the late 1950s floor covering in the majority of British homes took the form of linoleum or loose rugs. Carpet beating, whilst the rug was hung over the washing line, or sending the carpet away to be cleaned, with the inherent problems of colour bleeding and shrinkage, were the only known methods of cleaning. The ServiceMaster on-site carpet cleaning system was a novel idea which was initially repudiated by many as a fanciful notion! However, its universal acceptance has made wall-to-wall carpeting the norm rather than the exception. Again franchisees found the ServiceMaster franchise appealing because of the unique technology and know-how.

Similarly, the Dyno-Rod franchise was based upon sophisticated electromechanical drain clearing equipment. Prior to the introduction of the Dyno-Rod equipment, this task was the domain of a local plumber. The Dyno-Rod philosophy was to offer a unique service which was available 24 hours a day, 7 days a week; an attractive idea for the customer and potential franchisee.

The business lines of all three of the above companies were therefore quite distinct from anything else available in the market at that time. It was this very success that drew competitors into the field. The operations of ServiceMaster, Dyno-Rod and Wimpy have all been duplicated by rival franchise and non-franchise organizations.

Uniqueness

With uniqueness no longer a factor, these early pioneers had to seek other methods not only to attract franchisees but also to ensure continuing success in the market place. A number of changes were introduced, new marketing and selling programmes developed which in turn called for a revision of the organizational structures and administrative procedures, and so the business format evolved.

Potential franchisees are attracted to a business format franchise because it not only gives them access to a product or service, but also an entire business concept or blueprint. In addition, the franchisee is initiated and trained in running all aspects of the business according to the blueprint.

A business format franchise is marketed to the potential franchisee as a means of setting up in business with the support of an organization that has successfully carried out pilot operations which serve as a model. The business blueprint eliminates many of the risks inherent in a business start-up. This concept is quite different to that of the market for the first UK franchises.

In the business format franchise market, some of the more mature franchisors have been reducing their reliance on franchising. Wimpy has encountered serious competition from large capital-intensive outlets set up by the leading American fast-food company, McDonald's. Few individuals have the necessary capital to finance the scale of operation which Wimpy now see as essential for a successful franchise. In recent years therefore, much of their growth has been in company-owned outlets. Franchised outlets do, however, continue to play an important role in the Wimpy organization in the UK while McDonald's have very few franchised units in the UK. The majority were set up and continue to operate as company-owned restaurants.

The Body Shop

One of the greatest successes in the recent franchise boom in the UK has been the Body Shop franchise. The first Body Shop was opened in Brighton in 1976 by Anita Roddick to retail cosmetics produced from natural products. Its unique presentation of the goods and system of refillable bottles were important components in the success of the business. Having no further capital of their own, the proprietors turned to franchising in order to expand.

The Body Shop franchise proved extremely popular with potential franchisees through the success of the concept with the public. In 1984 the company was floated on the USM with 105 franchised outlets, 56 of which were abroad.

A number of well-known companies who previously operated through purely company-owned outlets, have in recent years expanded through franchising. Both Ryman, office supply retailers, and Sketchley, dry cleaners, have used franchising. Another area of rapid growth is in the domestic cleaning franchise. Women are increasingly being attracted back into the job market, and consequently seek reliable help with domestic chores. Molly Maid, the Maids, Poppies and Dial-A-Char all offer a domestic cleaning franchise.

The future

Franchising has an exciting future. During the 1980s it lost its tarnished image and association with pyramid selling. It now has a reputable trade association in the form of the BFA and looking forward to the 1990s, we predict a further period of growth of the franchise as a means of business expansion. In particular we see franchising in the 1990s developing in a number of ways.

First, the 1990s will see the continued use of franchising as a means of promoting an innovative product or service. Second, we envisage a growth in the popularity of franchising in the retail trade. There is a growing trend towards stores within stores, many of which are franchised. In addition, franchising will become increasingly strong in the service sector. This process has already started in the United States and the trend is likely to follow here. There are franchises in domestic cleaning, printing and accounting services and the possibilities in the service sector are vast. In the future it is likely that potential franchisees will seek franchisors who offer a better standard of advice and assistance in setting up their business than their competitors.

We also anticipate franchisees demanding a guaranteed turnover or level of profit before investing their capital. This may lead to franchisors initially opening outlets as company-owned operations in order to satisfy these demands. Having established that an outlet is profitable the franchisor may then offer the unit to a franchisee.

Traditionally in the UK, a franchisee has been responsible for acquiring the customers. In the future franchisees may demand or franchisors choose to provide assistance in establishing a market through a central marketing function. Many franchises were founded on the basis of obtaining economies of scale in a fragmented market. It is therefore a natural progression for the franchisor to promote the goods or service on behalf of the franchisee centrally. Indeed, as the number of franchisors in a particular market sector increases, the potential franchisee will be searching for the one offering the most attractive package in terms of profitability and likelihood of success. Marketing programmes will play an increasingly important role in assessing a franchise package.

Technological advance

Advancements in technology will also have a great influence in the future of the world of franchising. These are likely to involve the franchisors and bring them in closer contact with the franchisee. Retail businesses are increasingly using EPOS (electronic point of sale) equipment. In the future, franchisors may insist that franchisees invest in this equipment to link the retail store to the franchisor's warehouse. Thus, as sales are recorded on the franchisee's till, a record system at the franchisor's warehouse will ensure that supplies at the franchisee's premises are replenished. It will also allow information to be exchanged more rapidly between franchisee and franchisor.

By installing EPOS at all franchised outlets, franchisors could obtain immediate information on slow-moving items at one store and compare this to other outlets. The lack of sales could be remedied by central or local marketing depending on the circumstances. In addition the franchisor could control the timing of deliveries from suppliers to the central warehouse or individual outlets.

By investing in technology a franchisor may also serve customers who require central accounting and thus increase the market for franchisees. For example, a company may be looking for an organization which can provide commercial cleaning services to its geographically spread branches, but account for this through one invoice per month covering all sites. If a franchisor were to install networked computers in all franchised outlets, the information could be collected centrally and invoiced as required. A franchisor could also collect cash centrally; this would reduce the administration costs for the franchisee and guarantee the percentage of income at the time of cash receipt for the franchisor. It is possible then that we may witness a number of new entrants to the franchising world as the new technology and greater control over the franchised operation make franchising a more attractive alternative for would-be franchisors.

Economies of scale

Franchising has an exciting future. It will continue to serve businesses who are looking for economies of scale, but who operate in dispersed markets. Where customers seek a standardized service, the franchise will offer a cost effective method of expansion for the franchisor. We are likely to see the franchisee making greater demands on the franchisor for assistance in marketing and support and the franchisor looking for increased information and control through the use of increasingly advanced technology.

In this chapter we have briefly examined the history of franchising from the 'tied houses' of the early 1800s through the first generation car dealerships to the second-generation business format franchise boom of the late 1950s. Franchising in its current form is difficult to define precisely. In the text we have discussed the widely accepted definition of the British Franchise Association and looked at other possible franchise groupings, in particular the business format franchise.

We recognize the problems of grouping and suggest that attempts to classify franchises, other than by service sectors, are likely to cause confusion.

Just as the 'business format' evolved through market forces, we anticipate that franchising will continue to expand and respond to the challenge of change throughout the next decade.

Key points

- Franchises can vary from one-man businesses to large-scale capital investment projects.
- The British Franchise Association performs a key role in the industry.
- Franchising has largely overcome its troubled history.
- Growth prospects for the 1990s appear good.

2

What can be franchised?

Outline

This chapter looks at:

- the origins of a franchise
- the life cycle of a franchise
- the importance of a blueprint
- areas of franchise activity

In the first chapter of this book, we saw that franchising could be defined as a licence granted by the franchisor to a franchisee to operate a particular business using the franchisor's name where the franchisor provides assistance to the franchisee, exercises continuing control and receives periodical financial considerations from the franchisee, for the services provided.

If we look at this definition in the context of franchises which exist today, it would appear that almost any type or size of business can be franchised, from fast food to cleaning, from industrial products to personal services and from the small van-operated business to the large multinational chain, and yet many businesses have adopted the franchise system and failed. So what are the factors which determine whether a business is suitable for franchising and the basic criteria determining what can be franchised successfully? In order to answer these questions, we will look at the external factors which will affect the development of the franchise and the internal characteristics inherent in the franchise itself.

If we look at the history and development of franchising, we will see that external factors, such as the economy and political climate of a country, have a large part to play in determining what can be franchised.

In the USA the development of large-scale enterprises with

17

economic concentration in a geographical area was accompanied by a move towards tertiary activities where the main feature was the importance of the relationship with the end consumer.

Decentralization and the setting up of multiple outlets proved inadequate in handling the problems of supervision, personal motivation and the quality control expected in an advanced society.

Corporations

Corporations sought alternative means of retaining profitable control over outlying operations both in the domestic and foreign markets. In addition the economies of scale achieved through mass manufacturing and economic concentration produced a contradiction in the diseconomies of operating sales and servicing facilities over widespread geographical markets.

Franchising provided the means of retaining an element of control over those difficult-to-manage outlets. It also provided the opportunity for small enterprises to set up and become established through a shared involvement in the business.

The Singer Sewing Machine Co in the USA were the first to appreciate that their sophisticated manufactured product required back-up and advice from people committed to the local market who possessed the necessary skills.

At the turn of the century, the United States car industry quickly identified the problems of selling and servicing motor cars 3,000 miles away from the home base. The car, like the sewing machine, is sold in a highly individual transaction. Consumers do not buy something as costly as a car without due consideration. After-sales service is important but, very frequently also, the dealer purchases the old car, making the transaction even more complex. Car manufacturers preferred not to be involved in such highly individual transactions, nor did they want to carry stocks of second-hand vehicles, each having a variable local market price. They quickly moved into franchising.

These historical instances serve to demonstrate how a country's economy favours franchising and what is likely to be franchised. Franchising proves particularly suitable where geographically dispersed outlets serve small local markets with products which require a high level of customer care and attention. As countries move from a manufacturing-based to a service-based economy so customer awareness increases and places even greater demand on service at the local level.

Economic, political and geographical factors

Economic factors and geographically dispersed markets must also be accompanied by a political and cultural environment favourable to franchising. This has been the situation in Australia where franchising has grown rapidly. Conversely in Russia the political climate has not been favourable. The government there has concentrated its efforts on steering the economy through influencing the larger enterprise; small enterprises are either neglected or dismissed as not worth the effort required to influence the large numbers involved. Should the political climate continue to change, as in early 1990, we could well see a boom of franchise activity in the USSR, the most geographically dispersed of all countries.

Franchising did not totally solve the problem of servicing and supplying products to outlets which are widely dispersed over great distances. A number of US franchisors, including car manufacturers, resolved this by establishing a second layer in the franchise chain, variously referred to as 'main distributors', 'area franchisees', 'master franchisees', 'franchise co-ordinators' or other combinations. Whilst the exact details of operation vary between each company the master franchisee could be expected to buy into the system through the purchase of a number of franchised areas, stock or existing first line franchisees.

The role of the master franchisee was to develop the territory through the recruitment and establishment of franchisees with responsibility for their training and the distribution of goods or services to them. Compensation was made to the master franchisee through larger discounts on products and/or a percentage of the fees paid by franchisees.

The master franchise method is frequently used by franchisors to establish their system in foreign markets. ServiceMaster was first introduced into the UK through this method in 1958 when a master licence was sold, giving the exclusive rights to operate the

ServiceMaster system in Europe. Occasionally a number of master agreements have been used to obtain geographical coverage in the UK, with different master licence holders being appointed for Scotland, Northern England, Midlands, Southern, etc.

Other than as a means for overseas development, the master franchise system is seldom used in the UK, primarily because distances do not pose as big a problem as in the USA or Australia and also due to the possibility of it being misconstrued as a pyramid selling scheme.

Pace and direction

The direction and pace of franchise development in the UK has, to a large extent, influenced the type of business that could be franchised successfully. Franchising in the UK developed extremely slowly. Only four franchises were introduced in a decade, Wimpy in 1955, ServiceMaster in 1958, followed by Dyno-Rod and Kentucky Fried Chicken in 1965, and each was based on an American concept. It may be that others considering franchising at that time believed that a unique product was necessary to succeed. If we examine early UK franchises we see a pattern emerging. The first franchises relied on technical superiority and a unique product or service.

However, as competition appeared in the form of another franchise or non-franchised operation and copied the service or product, the original franchisors were forced to come to the defence of their franchisees and introduce systems to ensure that their prices were competitive in the market-place. They passed on to their franchisees the benefits of bulk buying and economies of scale. They also introduced marketing plans to boost sales and administrative systems to help reduce overheads. It was this pattern that led to the development of the type of franchise we see today – the business format franchise.

Figure 1 shows the development of a particular franchise and its attraction to potential franchisees: initially a technical uniqueness which declined as competition entered the market; the development of a format, marketing and business systems; the occasional technical boost; and the gradual and increasing recognition of the trading name.

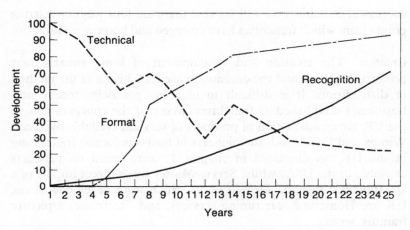

Figure 1 The development of an early franchise in the UK

So far in this chapter we have discussed the impact that the political, cultural, geographical and economic factors may have on the development of franchising. We will now look at the internal characteristics of the franchise and identify the basic criteria of the successful franchise. As we discussed earlier, franchising is a flexible system which can be readily adapted to suit a diversity of businesses, products and services. There are, however, a number of key characteristics which will determine whether the business can successfully be adapted to the franchise system. Firstly, and as with any business, the franchise will only succeed if it is profitable. Not only must it satisfy the needs of a consumer, the franchise has to meet the requirements of the other two principal parties, the franchisor and franchisee. Both the franchisor and franchisee require a return on their investment of time, money and resources while the customer seeks benefits and value for the price paid. If these three parties can be satisfied on a relatively long-term basis then the product or service can be franchised.

The product or service

Let us start with the product or service. It is true that the product or service does not have to be unique. If we look at some of the most successful franchises we will see that there are four ways or starting points from which franchises have emerged and become established:

Creation The creation and development of some entirely new product or service and the decision to use franchising as the method of distribution. It is difficult to identify, precisely, totally new businesses established as franchises. Many of the concepts new to the UK are an adaptation of products or services available overseas. Wimpy and Dyno-Rod, the pioneers of business format franchising in the UK, as discussed in chapter 1, were based on products available in the USA, whilst ServiceMaster was a direct import of a US franchise system. Two concepts which were developed in the UK are Hometune, car tuning services, and Fastframe, a picture framing service.

Adaptation Taking an existing product or service and adapting it for franchising. Wimpy, Dyno-Rod and many others have developed in this way.

Conversion Taking an existing, established business and turning company operated units into franchised outlets or expanding by franchising new outlets. A continually growing list includes estate agents, cleaning services, milk deliveries, double glazing, roof thatching, etc.

Importation Bringing in to the UK an existing franchise system from overseas, primarily the USA. Of the eight founder members of the BFA five were imports from North America and a sixth, Dyno-Rod, had a US Chairman and founder.

Whatever the product or service to be offered, there are a number of key questions to be asked. Is there a market for the product and sufficient demand in the market-place to ensure profitability both in the long and short term? The product or service must be able to withstand the test of time, and should not be based on a current fad or fashion. It must also have a universal market appeal rather than one that is restricted to a limited sector of the country or population. Having arrived at a product or service and established that a market exists, the next step is to set up a pilot outlet to test the concept.

A blueprint

The importance of a system – blueprint – plan or format has long since superseded the requirements for a unique product or service. Although those with original ideas may initially do well, the need to develop the systems and support rapidly is the key to long-term success. Once a business has been set up and tried and tested, it will obviously be easier to determine whether it will work in other markets and how the franchise should be structured. The franchisor must have a business which is successful in its own right and one for which others will be prepared to invest in the goodwill attached to a name or brand which is readily identifiable in the market-place. As the competition for franchisees increases, the franchisor will increasingly be required to offer a system that provides adequate support to his franchisee in terms of training and marketing assistance and financial advice. What can be franchised in today's market is as dependent on marketing programmes, which help to create demand, and administrative systems, to control quality and costs that will allow good returns on the investment of all parties, as any unique product or service. In addition, the product or service being franchised must be capable of being taught in a period of time that is acceptable to both franchisee and franchisor. For example, the training required to operate a limited menu restaurant, where the food is delivered having been previously prepared, can be measured in weeks. One of the many standard handbooks for a catering course, *Le Répertoire de la Cuisine*, contains around 7,000 recipes. The time taken to train a franchisee and staff to run a high quality à la carte French restaurant would be several years. The ability to set up a system or organization to support the franchisees in the long term and provide the required level of training, management and financial backing are the key ingredients in determining what can be franchised.

What can be franchised?

Answering the question 'What can be franchised?' is by no means simple. Whilst it is true that franchising offers a flexible approach which can be adapted to almost any type of business, product, service or market, success is by no means guaranteed. Franchising can only flourish in a favourable political and economic environment where the demand for the product or service and the size and characteristics of the potential market are sufficient to support long-term growth and profitability. But, whatever the product or service, the key to successful franchising depends on the existence of a proven business format: a business that has been tried and tested in the home market and one that offers an acceptable return to all three parties – franchisor, franchisee and consumer – on a long-term basis. The following list is by no means exhaustive but shows the range and wide variety of products and services which are currently being franchised today.

List of business activities known to be franchised

Automotive products and services

Automotive supplies, tyres, parts, tools, etc., axle alignment, car valeting, engine tuning, exhaust systems, rust proofing, sun-roof fitting, taxi hire, transmission repairs, tyre remoulding, vehicle cleaning, vehicle rental, vehicle repair, vehicle security, windscreen replacement, windscreen repair, chauffeur hire.

Business aids and services

Accountancy, bookkeeping, advertising services, information bureaux, display cards, postal centres, business brokerage, business counselling, computer bureaux, data processing, financial and debt counselling, job recruitment, temporary staff, office communications, photographic services, tax services, word processing bureaux.

Construction, home improvement and maintenance products and services

Air conditioning services, bathrooms and bath renovations, brick and stone pointing, ceiling cleaning, chimney lining, heat and energy conservation, condensation control, damp proofing, domestic boiler servicing, double glazing, draught exclusion, drain cleaning, electrical services, environmental cleaning, fireplaces, fitted kitchens, flooring materials and laying, garage doors and other doors, gutters, insulation, loft conversion, pavement surface repairs, plumbing, ready-mixed concrete, roof insulation and repair, tiles, timber preservation, water softening equipment.

Education services

Educational tuition, kindergartens, management skill training, secretarial training.

Entertainment, recreation, etc.

Hotels, whirlpools, adventure games indoors and outdoors.

Fast foods, restaurants and takeaways

Chicken, coffee, croissants, hamburgers, ice cream, orange juice, pancakes, pizzas, popcorn, potatoes, sandwiches, steaks, general restaurants.

Food stalls

Baked goods, confectionery, convenience stores, dairy produce, eggs, fish, grocery stores, health foods, fresh juices.

Health, medical and beauty care

Acupuncture and hypnotherapy, ambulance service, beauty centre, fitness health clubs and studios, hairdressing, optical goods, skin care, fitness equipment.

Household services

Carpet cleaning, curtain design and fitting, domestic cleaning services, furniture and fabric cleaning, furniture stripping and restoration, upholstery and vinyl repair.

Retailing (products and services not specified elsewhere)

Aquatic centres, bag stores and luggage, batteries, bridal wear, maternity wear, fashion wear, sports wear, ties, formal wear for sale and for hire, computer hardware and software, cosmetics and beauty products, dry cleaning, giftware, housewares and furnishings, knitting wools, instant print and copying shops, linen, original art, personalized badges, picture framing, photographic development, family histories, sewing machines, telephones and car telephone services, video films and equipment, window blinds.

Miscellaneous

Driving schools, equipment leasing and hire, estate agencies, publishing, local newspapers, etc., security equipment services, tent hire and instant accommodation hire, travel agencies, veterinary support services, wholesaling of carpets, biscuits, electrical and video equipment, will writing and storage.

Key points

- External factors determine what can be franchised in a particular country.
- Franchising developed slowly in the UK.
- The American influence is still strong.
- A wide variety of products and services are currently being franchised.

3

The advantages and disadvantages of franchising

Outline

This chapter looks at:

- the 'cloning' nature of franchising
- the advantages and disadvantages of franchising to:
  the franchisor
  the franchisee
  the consumer

Introduction

The first thirty years of the post-war era were characterized by a fascination with size. In one country after another, 'corporatist' policies saw state planners, big business and big unions developing economic strategies based, almost inevitably, on the premise that large size yields economies of scale, efficiency and wealth. In the late 1960s, however, politicians and economic planners began to wake up to the fact that *small* businesses were not merely a remnant of the first industrial revolution, doomed to extinction in the near future. Rather, large and small enterprises coexisted in a dynamic relationship of interdependence.

Since that time, the importance of the smaller business has become increasingly well understood. Goffee and Scase, in a recent book entitled *Entrepreneurship in Europe*, describe the small business owner as the 'popular hero' of our time. With unemployment in recent years running at levels unknown since the 1930s, and technological advance in the large firm sector leading often to, at best, 'jobless growth', politicians across the political spectrum are

27

increasingly looking to smaller businesses to create both jobs and wealth.

However, the interest in small business is not restricted to politicians and economic planners. As Goffee and Scase put it:

> On the one hand, changes in the broader ideological and cultural fabric of Western European countries have heightened peoples' expectations of independence and self-fulfillment [whilst], on the other hand, developments in technology and management practices have brought about tighter forms of employee control.

The tighter monitoring and control of so many jobs now appears at variance with growing desires for independence and autonomy, leading many people to start up their own businesses in an attempt to fulfil these ambitions. Although self-employment is a very demanding role and no business is completely free of external constraints, the personal involvement which so many crave is at least partially satisfied:

> Although most proprietors work long hours they are, nonetheless, free from the managerial control of others. Indeed, many see their businesses as extensions of their own personalities; by contrast, most employees feel constrained at work and are forced to shape their personalities according to the needs of their employer's businesses. (Goffee and Scase)

'Cloning' best practice

The conventional small firm population has, to date, been somewhat less successful than might have been hoped in terms of jobs and wealth creation. Not only do most small firms have a high initial risk of failure, most of those which do succeed create relatively few jobs. In fact, approximately two out of every three small businesses in Britain employ no one but the owner. The reasons for the failure to survive and grow are many. Small businesses are often chronically undercapitalized from the outset. Business ideas are not properly market tested. Pricing policies are flawed and financial control is often almost non-existent. All of these factors indicate that most small businessmen need outside help in getting established.

A major problem here is lack of knowledge and guidance where the small business is concerned. Governments and others have tried to help but with limited success. Professor David Birch in his much quoted (and also frequently misquoted) report on *The Job Generation Process* has made the point:

> It is no wonder that efforts to stem the tide of job decline have been so frustrating. . . . The firms that such efforts must reach are the most difficult to identify and the most difficult to work with. They are volatile. The very spirit that gives them their vitality and job generating powers is the same spirit that makes them unpromising partners for the development administrator.

Small businesses mistrust government and bureaucracy, no matter how well meaning. But franchising can and does embrace a link between the small business and the expertise and specialization that come with size, in a way that national governments have failed to achieve. Government aid is spread widely and thinly over large numbers of small businessmen who essentially select themselves for the role of entrepreneur, no matter how unsuited. In the franchise situation, in addition to other inherent advantages, there is a selection process which, whilst not perfect, weeds out many unsuitable candidates. Thus, franchising is designed as a method of 'cloning' success by duplicating a format based on established 'best practice'.

The remainder of this chapter summarizes the principal advantages and disadvantages claimed for franchising, reviewed from the respective standpoints of each of the principal parties involved – the franchisor, the franchisee and the consumer.

Advantages to the franchisor

- Franchising enables the franchisor to increase the number of distribution outlets for his organization's product or service for minimal capital investment. It is the franchisees who provide the capital with their investment stake in the business.
- Since the franchisee owns his own business he is assumed to be highly motivated to maximize profits. This situation may be compared with that of a manager of a retail outlet who is a direct employee of the parent company. Generally such a manager is on

a fixed salary (with possibly an element of bonus incentive incorporated) and lacks the extra incentive to succeed which may result from a personal financial investment in the business. A successful franchisee, with increasing profits, can be expected to contribute to the ultimate success of the franchisor.

- A franchised unit, being locally owned, is claimed to be readily accepted by the community as being a local business. It is not quite clear how far this is true in the UK, compared to the USA, since very often local people may not be aware that a franchised unit is in fact owner-managed. It would be interesting to know how many people realize that such a national institution as a widely known fast-food outlet is likely to be owner-managed as distinct from operating simply as one of a chain of company-owned outlets.

- The franchisor has limited payroll, rent and administrative overheads, because the very nature of the operation requires franchisees to be self-employed. Franchisees are themselves responsible for the staffing arrangements and operating costs of their own particular outlets.

- As well as the franchisor achieving a wider distribution network for his product or service, the nature of most franchise contracts ensures that franchisees are, in some measure, 'tied' to him. They are often obliged to purchase their equipment from or through the franchisor plus, as in the case of a fast-food franchise, the necessary ingredients that actually go to make up the final product. Since the franchise name is a protected trade name, the franchisor knows that no other operation can freely adopt and benefit from the selling power established through its reputation. It is also a name associated with an established product or service available wherever the customer visits an outlet which, in turn, is readily identifiable in terms of its structural design, physical layout and general presentation (certainly in the case of a franchise where the outlet is visited by the customer direct).

Disadvantages to the franchisor

- It has been claimed that company-owned units tend to be more profitable to the parent company than franchised outlets. In other words, whilst franchised outlets may allow a company to expand its distribution system quickly and cheaply, because the franchisor only receives a percentage of gross profits, these outlets may in fact be less profitable to him than if they were owned outright and simply managed by an employee-manager.

- It may be difficult for the franchisor to exercise tight control over franchisees simply because they are not employees of the franchisor and cannot be so closely supervised. The poor reputation of one outlet, in terms of product quality or service, can be damaging to the general trade name and reputation of the franchisor and, in turn, the whole franchise organization.

- A franchisor cannot always be certain that any franchisee is declaring his true level of business activity. Some franchisors employ a central accounting system to combat this, though no system can be expected to be totally successful in this respect.

- If for any reason an employer is unhappy with the performance of one of his managers, he can either dismiss or transfer him. If a franchisor believes a franchised outlet is not being run at maximum efficiency, there appears little he can do as long as the franchisee is operating within the terms of his contract. A franchisee may lose some of his initial motivation once a desired lifestyle has been attained, yet his geographical area of operation may have much potential yet to be exploited. In such a situation the needs of franchisor and franchisee may conflict but the franchisor cannot simply remove the franchisee and replace him with a more efficient operator.

- The management of a franchising company is limited in its flexibility. Ordinary companies can move in any direction to exploit market potential, when a modified selling strategy is required. However, to bring about such changes can be a lengthy and cumbersome operation when dealing with individually owned franchised outlets. Any changes need to be carefully handled to avoid conflicts stemming from perceived threats to the franchisee's independence.

- There may be problems of information feedback from the franchisee to the franchisor. This can result from the franchisee's desire for independence or simply from channels of communication not being as well developed as they might be in company-owned and managed units.

- The franchisor is faced with a paradox. The franchise method of business tries to capitalize on the personal attention and service that characterize the owner-managed business. However, the franchisor's need for a standardized product or service, together with uniform presentation, needed to give customers a sense of reliability and dependability, clashes with this objective.
- The franchisor may have difficulty in recruiting suitable franchisees who (1) see franchising as an attractive method of doing business, (2) are motivated by the prospect of self-employment, and (3) have the necessary capital available for investment.

Advantages to the franchisee

- It is possible, via franchising, for an individual to run his own small business yet share in the advantages and economies available to a large company. The franchisee's lack of basic or specialized knowledge is compensated by a training programme organized by the franchisor (although not all franchisors organize full-time training programmes, most give at least 'on the job' guidance). In theory at least, the equipment, ingredients, etc., that go to make up the end product or service are pre-tested and proven and can be purchased more cheaply via the franchisor than if the franchisee directly purchased them himself. The franchisor can supply professional managerial advice and guidance to overcome the problems that any small business is likely to face.
- The franchisee sells a product or provides a service with a known trade name. If the product is already a proven success, then the franchisee can concentrate merely on the day-to-day running of his business rather than being preoccupied with promotion of the product. Most franchisors undertake both national and local advertising campaigns to keep franchisees' products or services firmly in the public mind. Promotion on such a scale would be beyond the scope of an individual or small business.
- It is claimed that a franchisee needs less capital than if he were to start a business independently because of the assistance that the franchisor provides. He is helped with site selection, problems of planning, staff training and getting the business open and

running smoothly. He may also be assisted in the task of obtaining finance for his acquisition of the business. Investment fees involved in entry into a franchise can be quite high and it could be argued that for the sum involved, one could start a business successfully without the obligations imposed by a franchisor.

- Because the franchisee is assisted by the franchisor it should mean that his risk is reduced. Of course this does not mean he is not exposed to any risk at all. Furthermore, a franchised unit is a small business and franchisees frequently work hard and work long hours in order to be successful. Most franchisors are careful to state that franchisees should be prepared to work harder than they may have ever done before.

- The franchisee should receive the benefit of continuous research and development programmes to improve the business and keep pace with consumer demand allied to technological change.

- The franchisee obtains market information which he would not otherwise get. Most franchisors employ market researchers to take stock of the prevailing state of the market and relevant information is circulated to franchisees, often via a monthly newsletter.

- Many franchisees operate within a defined territory which involves the franchisor giving an undertaking not to set up another competing outlet within a given geographical radius. This can, however, lead to problems. If a franchisee can only cope with a proportion of the market open to him, it might pay the franchisor to open a further outlet to take in the additional market. The whole market would then be split between two outlets and the owner of the original might find that his reduced share of the market has left him under-utilized. What in fact often happens in such a situation is that an additional outlet is offered to the original franchisee so that he runs both outlets, probably with the help of hired staff. Alternatively, he may sell one of them. Either way, business increases and franchisor–franchisee conflict is minimized. However, there is nothing to prevent other franchisors of similar products and services from moving into an area that appears particularly attractive and lucrative. Depending on the size of the market there may be room for both. This was frequently not the case, however, in the 1960s boom in launderettes which witnessed competing franchisors opening new outlets sometimes within a few yards of each other.

- The franchisee is independent in so far as he owns his business and its success is to an extent dependent upon the amount of work he puts into it.

Disadvantages to the franchisee

- The control exercised by the franchisor to regulate the way in which a product or service is presented to the consumer may leave little opportunity for a franchisee to impose his own personality on his business. Of course, some centralized control is necessary to ensure product quality and consistency, but if the franchisee is given no scope for innovations and ideas of his own, he may begin to wonder what is the point of owning his own business. He may come to feel that he is merely managing a company-owned business on a piece-work contract. The franchisee, if he is to succeed, must accept that much of his success is achieved by virtue of the franchisor.
- Should the trade name of the franchise company become tarnished, perhaps through mismanagement by the franchisor, or the shortcomings of other franchisees, then there is a possibility that the franchisee may suffer simply because he is seen by the public as a representative of the franchise organization in question.
- The services provided by the franchisor may constitute a heavy expense to the franchisee. The franchisee may be obliged to purchase equipment and ingredients from the franchisor which he could have bought more cheaply from other sources.
- There is a possibility that the franchise agreement may not fulfil the franchisee's initial expectations, either in terms of anticipated sales turnover, or in terms of the franchisor fulfilling his obligations. It is also possible that, through franchisor mismanagement, the company could go bankrupt.
- The existing franchisor may sell the entire franchise as a going concern. This will result in a new franchisor taking control and policies and procedures may change radically, not necessarily to the liking of existing franchisees. Decisions as to which franchisees

will still retain ownership of their own individual outlet(s) may result in a period of turbulence and uncertainty.

- On the death of a franchisee, a spouse may inherit, though the right of a spouse or the deceased's children to take over the running of the franchise outlet may be problematic and should not necessarily be taken for granted. It is possible, depending on the terms of the contract, that a sale may be obliged.
- A franchise is usually based upon a narrowly specialized product or service. In the absence of a diversified business base, it is always possible that technological advances, legal changes and/or consumer tastes, etc., could threaten the business.

Advantages to the consumer

- Some franchises offer an extended hours service to the consumer. Franchisees are aware that this may be a condition of their contract and will make the necessary provisions. The totally independent small businessman is not bound by agreements to provide such a high level of service, and indeed his resources may not be sufficient.
- Franchisees, as owner-managers, should be able to offer the consumer a highly personal service.
- Although all franchised outlets are separate and independent, the consumer can locate them under a single trade name. He can apply his knowledge of one outlet to all others because of uniform presentation and consistent standards of quality.
- Conversely, if the consumer is dissatisfied with the product or service he need not waste his time and money trying out the other outlets operating under the same trade name.
- Many small businesses run into financial difficulties and go into liquidation. Should a consumer need to return for further service (or indeed if he is dissatisfied with previous work) the small operator may have disappeared. A franchise organization supports its outlets so that even if a particular outlet closes then it is still possible to contact the parent company. It is claimed that franchised businesses have a lower failure rate than other small businesses but, as yet, there is little hard evidence for this assertion (see chapter 8).

- Small business is kept alive by franchising. It provides opportunities for the would-be small businessman or woman and maintains diversity of choice for the consumer in a period of increasing business concentration.

Disadvantages to the consumer

- Franchising can act to remove elements of competition and therefore consumer choice. Franchisees usually have protected territories and operate with uniform prices recommended by the franchisor. Franchisees are usually considered to be independent but the truly independent businessman can decide his own price for the product or service he presents to the consumer and has greater flexibility to adapt it to the needs of the individual consumer.
- Franchisees may lack managerial skills and/or training. This may result in administrative inefficiencies which manifest themselves in the quality of the service to the consumer. Such problems may be magnified when the franchisee is called upon to recruit and train his own employees. This may violate consumer expectations built up through contact with other outlets licensed by the franchisor.

In conclusion

In this section, it is evident that certain points are raised more than once under different headings and, further, that some of the points raised could quite easily be challenged or even contradict one another. Of course, some points are a benefit or drawback to *all* the parties, franchisor, franchisee and consumer. For example, high personal involvement on the part of the franchisee will normally increase both his income and personal satisfaction, but equally the franchisor will receive more profits and knows that the outlet is increasing its goodwill while the consumer receives quality service. But advantages or drawbacks for one of the parties may be the opposite for other parties.

Some of the assumptions underlying the alleged advantages of franchising as a type of business operation are questionable, as the earlier discussion has implied. In particular, some of the assumptions seem less applicable to Britain than the United States where they may have originated. For example, the idea that because a franchised business is operated by a member of the local community this will make it more popular among potential customers seems questionable in Britain. In many of Britain's urban areas, the American notion of community with close personal connections among people living within a locality simply does not apply. Further, while the ordinary American may well be quite familiar with franchising as a form of semi-independent enterprise, the British public are still less likely to be aware that the outlet is franchised and may simply assume that it is managed as a part of a chain.

The claim that franchised outlets are less profitable than directly managed outlets, made by some franchisors, is also questionable. This may be true in terms of absolute levels of profit but direct management means a much higher capital investment by the franchisor so that profit, as a return on capital, may well be lower than from franchised outlets.

The most serious weakness of many claims and counterclaims concerning franchising has been the sheer lack of empirical research underpinning it. Even in the United States, where franchising is an established part of the economy, research is still sparse and the results sometimes questionable.

Key points

- The interests of franchisor, franchisee and consumer may coincide.
- The interests of these three key parties may, on occasions, be in competition.
- Some of the claims made in this area are still vague and open to debate.

4

Becoming a franchisee

Outline

This chapter looks at:

- questions for would-be franchisees to put to franchisors
- who becomes a franchisee?
- sources of pre-entry advice
- prior experience related to success

Introduction

Franchisees come from a wide variety of backgrounds and range from university graduates to those who leave school at the earliest opportunity. What unites them is the idea of running a business of their own with the safety net of a larger company's know-how and resources.

Perhaps somewhat surprisingly, research shows that, in many ways, the typical franchisee is rather similar to the conventional independent small business owner. For instance, around a half of all franchisees have either had previous experience of self-employment or, alternatively, had parents who were self-employed.

There are fewer women in franchising than amongst the conventionally self-employed and this is somewhat surprising since franchising seems an ideal way for women to increase their share of self-employment opportunities.

Taking the franchise route

One reason people opt for the franchise route to working for themselves is that previous employment did not prepare them for self-employment. For example, working for a large company tends to produce fewer people who end up working for themselves, perhaps because large firm specialization does not give the all-round experience which lends itself to running a small business.

A franchise should substitute for this lack of experience by offering a proven business package with continuing support. It does much the same for those who have business skills but lack a business idea.

It should be understood by potential franchisees, however, that no business is totally risk free. Although compared with the conventional independent small business the survival rate of franchises is probably superior, failures do still occur.

Besides the benefits of a tried and tested business package, there are additional reasons why the small franchised enterprise should be less failure prone. For instance, many conventional small businesses go to the wall because they are hopelessly undercapitalized. In a reputable franchise this should not happen because the franchisor knows the likely costs and can often secure better loan facilities from banks.

Also, many small businesses fail simply because they have no proper financial and management control systems. Their pricing and overhead apportionment, for instance, is often based on guesswork. With a franchise, such systems should be part of the basic business format.

Just as franchisors vet applicants carefully, individuals thinking about this form of self-employment ought to ask themselves if they really are personally well suited.

Franchising may be a 'protected' form of business but it still requires hard work, long hours and as much get-up-and-go as any other small business. It also requires someone who can work for themselves and yet also work harmoniously with another host business.

Some franchises have fairly steep entry costs which rule them out for many people contemplating a small business. For instance, Wimpy in early 1989 were asking for a minimum investment of £450,000 but there were others on offer for under £10,000. Anyone deciding which franchise to go for should ask some basic questions to reduce the chances of making a serious mistake at this stage.

Questions to ask the franchisor

Key questions to put to the franchisor include the following:

- Is the franchise company a member of the British Franchise Association? This franchise industry trade association vets companies before admitting them to membership. Obviously some very good companies, for their own good reasons, prefer not to join but, none the less, membership can generally be counted in a company's favour.
- Are other franchisees successful using the format that you are considering? Potential investors should visit at least two existing outlets, preferably without the franchisor present, to talk to existing franchisees. These outlets should be freely selected from a complete list of existing outlets and should not be selected by the franchisor.
- Is the franchisor's long-term success dependent upon the success of franchisees? An ethical franchisor should be willing to take an income related to the franchisee's own success rather than demanding a *fixed* royalty or service fee.
- Is the franchisor selective in picking franchisees? Any shady operator interested only in short-term gain is likely to accept almost anyone willing to part with money.
- What would you get back if you decided to terminate your contract or in the event of your death? In a good franchise operation, an outlet that has been developed into a flourishing small business can be sold as a going concern or inherited by descendants subject only to a minimum of conditions which protect the franchisor's legitimate interests in the transaction.
- Is the figure you are told you will need to invest the total figure required to get you started or a minimum figure? Sometimes, sizeable amounts of loan capital and equipment rentals may also have to be found, putting a heavy repayment burden on the new franchisee. Also, a franchisor who does not readily give clear investment information from the outset may not be an ideal partner for the continuing business relationship that lies at the heart of a franchise.
- What is your estimate of the future potential of the franchise? Is demand for the product or service offered likely to be maintained

or, hopefully, increased? Some franchises that have been offered attempt to exploit a fad or fashion, but public taste has switched to something else leaving franchisees with a worthless business.

- Do the prospects for success appear just 'too good to be true'? If so, they almost certainly are. Promises of 'success beyond your wildest dreams' are invariably just that – dreams.

Most bogus or unethical franchises in the past have not been difficult to spot. Having said that, they have often not experienced too much difficulty in getting at least a number of people to part with their life savings. If you have substantial doubts, back off and find another franchise.

Readers who find this chapter of particular interest will find some of the key issues elaborated in chapter 6 (The Franchise Relationship) and chapter 7 (Working Out If Franchising is Right For You). However, for the moment, those considering taking up a franchise will find interesting the results of research related to this area.

Who becomes a franchisee?

Much of what is known about the question of who becomes a franchisee stems from research. Two major in-depth research projects into franchising with particular emphasis on the franchisee have been conducted in recent years at the Polytechnic of Central London. The first was based on three of the eight companies which founded the British Franchise Association in 1977 – Wimpy International (fast food); Dyno-Rod (drain cleaning and hygiene services) and ServiceMaster (carpet, upholstery and allied cleaning services).

In the second project, four companies were studied – Hometune (mobile car tuning), Prontaprint (high-speed printing services), Servowarm (central heating installation and servicing) and Ziebart (vehicle rust-proofing). The two projects, between them, involved over 400 respondents: 28 franchisors and 380 franchisees.

Amongst a detailed analysis of the characteristics of franchisees, the most remarkable finding was the very high level of experience of prior self-employment. The figures here were both high and consistent (see exhibit 1). The figures for respondents with previous

Franchise	Franchisees PSE* (%)	Fathers PSE* (%)	Both PSE* (%)	Franchisee or father PSE* (%)
Hometune	23.9	35.2	7.0	52.1
Prontaprint	32.8	35.9	15.6	53.1
Servowarm	53.1	37.5	25.0	65.6
Ziebart	33.3	43.8	18.8	58.3
ServiceMaster	16.1	16.1	0.0	32.2
Dyno-Rod	35.5	25.8	12.0	48.4
Wimpy	48.1	44.2	19.2	73.1

*PSE: Previously self-employed

Exhibit 1 History of previous self-employment amongst franchisees and fathers

first-hand experience of self-employment were between 33 per cent and 36 per cent overall for both projects and the figure for those with *either* direct experience *or* second-hand exposure via one or more parents was exactly 55 per cent on each occasion. The first of these figures is also corroborated by American research. Given that such a large proportion came from this background, additional interest is focused on the issue of the franchisor–franchisee relationship – on the accommodation of the franchisor's desire for standardization and control and the franchisee's quest for independence and autonomy.

Age

As is the case for conventional small businessmen, franchisees appear most likely to take up their franchised businesses when they are in their 20s or 30s. Approximately 35 per cent set up in their 30s compared to 30 per cent in their 20s and 23 per cent in their 40s. There appears little support for any suggestion that franchisees enter their business ventures at notably different stages in their careers than conventional small businessmen. In fact, the evidence is that the type of business (business sector) is more important here than whether it is franchised or not.

For instance, in the most expensive of the four franchises in the second project (Prontaprint), only 17 per cent started up in their 20s, compared with 45 per cent from the lowest entry cost franchise (Hometune). The franchise with the highest percentage setting up in their 40s (Servowarm) also had the highest percentage of previously self-employed (53 per cent) for whom franchising was their second or subsequent attempt at self-employment. Thus, where distinct patterns did emerge, they appeared to be explained by a variety of factors, such as capital requirements and previous career histories. Also, it is worth remarking on the sheer spread of ages of incoming franchisees. In the second research project, three out of the four franchises had recruited franchisees in their 60s (information on this issue is not available from the first project).

Marital status

The value of assistance from a spouse to the successful running of a small business is becoming increasingly realized. There are several ways in which this can come about, either inside the business or even outside it (e.g. by supplementing the family income). Only one of the franchises formally required a prospective franchisee's spouse to take part in the interview process but, in the others, it was not uncommon for the spouse to attend at least one of the interviews.

Nearly 90 per cent of the franchisees were married and nearly 70 per cent had spouses involved to a greater or lesser extent in the day-to-day running of their franchise. In the home-based franchises (Hometune, Servowarm and ServiceMaster), the figure was in the region of 70–80 per cent whilst the others averaged around 50 per cent. In conventional small businesses, it has been noted that there is a tendency for wives to withdraw from the business as it expands. However, this did not appear the case with franchise businesses. In all, a third of spouses had employment outside the franchise but more than half of these helped in the franchise as well.

Education

Ozanne and Hunt, in their franchise research in the US, noted an 'unexpectedly high level of formal education amongst a study of fast food franchisees with only 10% not completing high school at one extreme and a similar proportion obtaining post-graduate qualifications at the other'. In the UK research, both projects showed half of the franchisees as having had either a selective state or private education, thus rendering them characteristically different from the population as a whole.

There was a distinct pattern (and positive correlation) linking buy-in cost of the franchise to likelihood of (1) having attended a selective state school, (2) having had a private education and (3) having left school with some form of qualification. As might be expected, those with manual worker fathers were the most likely to have attended a non-selective state school and to have left without any formal qualifications. Those from upper white-collar backgrounds were the most likely to have left school with qualifications, although they were more likely to have attended non-selective state schools than those whose fathers were self-employed.

Nearly two-thirds of franchisees undertook some form of college education after leaving school. This was usually on a part-time basis in the case of the low-cost franchise, Hometune, but most commonly full-time in the case of the highest cost franchise, Prontaprint. Franchisees who had attended grammar schools were more than three times as likely to have subsequently studied full-time as those who attended non-selective state schools.

Pre-entry advice

It is a conventional wisdom that many people who stage an entry into business do so with a minimum of planning and advice and their general approach is essentially haphazard. In some respects, the franchisees in the current research replicated this – in both projects, only one-fifth investigated more than one franchise opportunity.

However, the level of pre-entry investigation undertaken by franchisees appeared related to a number of factors. First was the level of franchise investment required – 38 per cent of Prontaprint respondents and 31 per cent from Dyno-Rod considered more than one franchise opportunity whereas from Hometune and ServiceMaster the figures were only 11 per cent and 13 per cent respectively. There was, however, a remarkable change over time. For instance, of the Hometune respondents who had taken their franchises during the two years prior to interview, over 40 per cent had considered more than one franchise, indicating a general trend towards greater awareness.

Respondents who bought existing franchise outlets were less likely than those setting up from scratch to consider other franchises. It is, however, possible that these people were more concerned to buy an ongoing business than they were to buy a franchise *per se* and they may thus have considered other business propositions, albeit non-franchised.

In the case of all four franchises in the second project, between 70 per cent and 90 per cent sought professional advice from a third party. Again the distribution was as might be expected, with respondents from the higher investment figure franchisees being more likely to seek advice. The most important source of advice was solicitors (56 per cent) followed by bank managers (48 per cent) and accountants (40 per cent). Less than 10 per cent sought advice from other professional sources. There was some evidence that, when individual franchises were experiencing serious trading difficulties, incoming franchisees were considerably less likely to have taken third party advice which appeared to be linked to lower levels of encouragement to do so by franchisors.

The tendency for prospective franchisees to seek third party advice appeared to be increasing over time. However, less than 20 per cent of the franchisees studied felt that their advisers had been very knowledgeable about franchising – more than 60 per cent felt that they were definitely *not* knowledgeable. By far the most knowledgeable and reliable advice came from a non-professional source – existing franchisees. Over 95 per cent of those reporting on this question felt that they had been supplied with accurate information. This source of advice was regarded as essentially neutral with most being given neither encouragement or discouragement.

The importance of the bank manager to franchisees did not stop at advice. The first of the two projects being reported here showed that 45 per cent obtained funding assistance from the clearing banks when starting up. The second project, some time later, indicated that this figure had risen to over 50 per cent. In fact, 42 per cent claimed to have raised over one quarter of their total start-up requirements from the clearing banks and, of these, 25 per cent claimed to have raised over half.

Prior work experience and franchisee profitability

At the time of entry into franchising, franchisees from the various companies varied considerably in terms of previous educational background and work experience. The level of capital investment required to enter the respective franchises correlated quite closely with certain franchise characteristics. For instance, in the second project, nearly 35 per cent of Prontaprint franchisees had degrees or degree-level professional qualifications compared with 7 per cent in the case of Hometune. The spread of occupational posts held prior to entry into franchising reflected this with Hometune respondents being far more likely to have been involved in manual work than Prontaprint respondents (in the first project, the same contrast was apparent between ServiceMaster and Dyno-Rod respondents).

Prior experience in the operational line of the franchise is often seen as undesirable. Franchisor executives tended to prefer people from outside their industry with no preconceived ideas or bad habits which might interfere with the franchisor's training programme or contaminate other franchisees.

Research into fast-food franchisees in the US indicates that those *with* prior experience tend to be at least modestly more successful. This research also pointed to a link between income levels achieved in previous employment and success as a franchisee.

An attempt to yield information on profitability in the UK, by asking respondents to state their levels of satisfaction with their profitability, yielded fairly high levels of satisfaction (60 per cent were 'fairly satisfied' or 'very satisfied'). Nearly 80 per cent of respondents were willing to state the income levels taken from their franchise in the year before interview and this data was compared with official statistics on earnings levels for employees in the occupational groups of which the franchisees had previously been members. The resulting analysis indicated that one third were drawing less than they might have received as employees. However, it is quite possible that, in the relatively early years of establishing a business, many franchisees were deliberately retaining as much money in the business as possible. Also, this form of analysis makes no allowance for the fringe benefits associated with self-employment, nor some of the non-monetary rewards and satisfactions.

Key points

- A sizeable minority of franchisees have been previously self-employed.
- Pre-entry research can pay good dividends.
- The best source of information for franchisees is other franchisees.

5

Becoming a franchisor

Outline

This chapter looks at:

- franchising as a route to business expansion
- researching the potential market
- sources of franchise revenue
- services provided to the franchisee
- training and operating manuals

In previous chapters we have discussed franchising, its definition and the type of business that can be franchised. It is now time to turn our attention to one of the key players in the franchise agreement – the franchisor. A franchisor is an individual, company or partnership that has chosen franchising as an appropriate system through which to distribute goods or service. In this chapter we will look at the reasons why people or companies decide to take the franchise route and become franchisors, and identify the key steps to be taken to ensure that the franchise operation is launched successfully from the initial business and review through to the development of the right package to attract and support the franchisees.

A business seeking growth will find that franchising provides a number of advantages and benefits which are not available through other, more traditional, methods of business expansion.

First, it allows the number of outlets to be increased more rapidly and with less capital costs than other methods. The capital expenditure for opening new outlets is borne by the franchisee thereby reducing the financing needs of the franchisor.

It can achieve a greater market penetration and prove a safer and more effective method of entering new markets where local knowledge and skills are important, particularly overseas.

Franchisees tend to be more motivated than employees, often resulting in higher volumes of sales from their outlets than achieved with a salaried manager.

Franchising also allows the franchisor to save or reduce his overhead cost at both branch and head office levels. As the franchisee is responsible for his own staff, less supervision is required and administrative costs are lower.

Cost effective

It is clear from the above that franchising can be an efficient and cost effective way for the franchisor to expand his business but, whatever the reason for deciding to franchise, there are several essential steps to take if the franchise is to be effectively launched and for it to enjoy continuing success. The setting up and establishment of a franchise business involves two distinct operations; one, running the core business; and two, establishing and running a franchise system.

If a business is to succeed as a franchise it needs to be successful and be capable of being seen to be successful in its own right. Franchising is not an instant cure for a sick business. It will initially add to rather than resolve any problems there may be with cash flow, profitability or management.

Managing any business requires the skills and specialized knowledge of that business. The skills may be in manufacturing, buying, design, engineering, merchandising, marketing, etc., but will generally be specific to that industry. The potential franchisor must clearly understand and be successful in his own business before considering establishing a franchise operation which will require additional skills in management and administration.

A successful franchisor has to recruit, train, develop, direct, control, retrain and retain franchisees.

Few successful

Only a few franchisors have been successful in establishing more than one additional franchise system and many have failed often with disastrous consequences. Similarly many tried-and-tested businesses have been unsuccessful when following the franchise route because they have been unable to develop or acquire the skills necessary to run a franchised business.

It can be seen from the above that before a franchising programme can be implemented a proven business must exist, and the franchisor needs to acquire extra skills to meet the training and management needs of a larger, dynamic, more independent organization which may be widely dispersed.

Given that a business exists and that that business is proven, the next step is to conduct a complete review of the business, market-place and competitive situation.

Business review

The first point to consider is the current established business. Is there a sufficient, widespread need or demand for the product or services? Is this demand likely to continue or is it seasonal or a fad? What is the long-term potential? Are there likely to be regional differences in demand? Is the product or service price sensitive?

The market

What is its size? Now; in 5 years; in 10 years.
How is it distributed?
What is the current market share?
What is the customer type (target market)?
Who is the competition?

Distinctive competence/resources

What are we good at?
What are we known for?
What financial resources are available?
What human resources are available?
What management skills do we have or need?
What technical skills do we have or need?
What marketing skills do we have or need?

Such questions and the responses are designed to ensure that the basic business is sound and has a long-term future, and that the financial and human resources are available to invest in and sustain a franchise venture. Once the review has been completed, the prospective franchisor can move on the the next steps:

The pilot operation	Developing and proving the franchise format
The offer	
Recruiting franchisees	Establishing the elements of the package
Supporting franchisees	Formalizing the process of selection
Protecting franchisees	Planning the organization
	Counselling and research

The pilot operation

First of all, it is important for the franchisor to establish and run a successful pilot operation.

As franchising will require investment and risk taking from franchisees, it can be appreciated that the more tangible the evidence of their likely success the better. Potential franchisees today have more independent advice and information available than ever before. They will tend to view with suspicion any franchise opportunity that does not follow the basic recommendations given by banks, accountants, consultants, lawyers and books. Predominant among the recommendations is that the franchisor should have successfully operated a pilot operation for a minimum period of one year.

In chapter 2 we identified franchising as a method of 'cloning' success by duplicating a format based on established best practice.

The purpose of the pilot operation is to develop that 'best practice' in all aspects of the business.

Operations Layout, staffing, cooking/cleaning/serving/maintaining, opening hours, levels of service, products and services to be offered, acceptability, location . . .

Administration Management, accounting, VAT, training, compliance with local by-laws, building and fire regulations, health and safety at work, planning, ordering, invoicing, debt collection, cash management . . .

Marketing Design, identification, promotion, press and public relations, merchandising, promotional literature, specifications, menus, signs, logos, advertising . . .

In the pilot operation, and all subsequent operations, it is advisable to keep the systems, programmes and operating procedures as simple as possible. Once established they should be written up to form the basis of the operating manuals.

Where premises will be a feature of the franchise, the location of the pilot operation must be as representative of future proposed franchised outlets as possible. No matter how desirable or profitable pilot shops in the centre of London or other major cities are, they will not prove that the concept will work in other less populated, less cosmopolitan areas.

Whilst perhaps difficult with the first outlet, pilot operations should not receive an excess of attention, help or support from head office. A strict record should be kept of all support and promotion to ensure that those methods which work can be duplicated in subsequent outlets and ensure that those which do not work are not continued or repeated.

A very important function of the pilot operation is to establish the level and format of the payments franchisees will make to the franchisor. This includes both the initial fee and subsequent payments.

Initial payments

Initial payments may be made from the capital resources the franchisee has amassed; however, consideration must also be given to borrowed funds. Most franchisees borrow money to buy a franchised business. The business must prove itself capable of meeting both the interest and capital repayments of any debt incurred plus, of course, all ongoing costs.

Traditionally the first generation franchisors made their profit from the sale of their products – motor cars, sewing machines and beer. The brewers also have income from charging a rent, loosely based on the turnover of the public house.

The tendency in modern-day, business format franchising is for the franchisor to depend less on the sales of supplies and more on a management services fee as the main source of income. One of the reasons for this is as a result of external pressures and market forces. Early franchisors followed the traditional view that the franchisees were seen as distributors of the franchisors' products and therefore insisted on being the sole supplier. This tied arrangement has been criticized and abused. It is currently the subject of much discussion at a governmental level, particularly with reference to the brewing, petrol and oil industries.

A franchisor may receive revenue from a variety of sources.

1 Income from company owned outlets
2 A mark up on initial materials and supplies
3 A mark up on the continuing supply of goods
4 Discounts or commissions from suppliers
5 An initial fee
6 A premium (on premises)
7 Income from rent (leased or sub-leased)
8 Income from leasing equipment/vehicles
9 Interest on loans
10 A management service (or other named) fee using any of the following formulae:
   (a) a percentage of the franchisee's sales
   (b) a percentage of profit
   (c) a fixed monthly sum
11 A marketing fee

The general concept of business format franchising is one of fair dealing between the franchisor and franchisee where both grow because of each other's efforts. All of the above can be considered as viable methods of sharing the costs and profits when taken in this context. The running of the pilot operation will establish the right mix for both parties.

Revenue from company outlets will, in the beginning, probably be the sole source of income. Most franchisors continue to operate company units after the franchise is well established. They fulfil a useful role as a training facility, as well as enabling the franchisor to test and refine new ideas. They should also be profitable in their own right.

Mobile franchises

Mobile franchises, such as ServiceMaster, Dyno-Rod and Hometune are concerned with reliability and a standard, identifiable fleet of vehicles. In addition the cost of a vehicle in this type of franchise can be disproportionate in terms of the franchise offer. For these reasons a number of mobile franchised businesses offer favourable, fleet rate, leasing arrangements.

A mark-up or discount on initial and/or ongoing supplies will be necessary if the franchisor has to carry stock and distribute it to the franchised outlets. The ability to buy in quantity and gain from economies of scale should be beneficial to both parties. Where premises are needed for the franchise, the franchisor may buy or take the head lease, as landlords will be more willing to lease to the larger franchisor organization. The franchisor will usually expect the franchisee to pay any premiums that are required.

A number of franchisors make voluntary loans to their franchisees and will expect a fair rate of interest to be paid. It was only nine years ago, in 1981, that franchising was formally recognized by the banking community when Barclays and one of the other appointed franchise managers. Today most of the major banks have centrally located managers with specific franchising responsibilities. As a result of this interest the practice of the franchisor lending to the franchisee is declining.

To recruit, train and establish any franchisee in an outlet costs money. The franchisor will wish to recover some if not all of these costs by charging an initial fee.

Initial fee

It is occasionally suggested that the initial fee should represent some percentage of the total initial cost of buying the franchise. There is no logical reason why this should be the case and indeed the enormous range of the set-up costs of a franchise, from £6,000 for a van-operated business to £12 million for a hotel, may suggest the opposite.

In establishing the initial fee it is important to identify the services which will be provided. The following is a list of the initial services which are usually provided by the franchisor.

1 Evaluating and finding a potential site and/or identifying an area
2 Assistance with lease negotiation or sub-leasing
3 Assistance with vehicle selection, financing or leasing
4 Corporate identity package
5 Interior layout and design schemes
6 Advice and assistance on opening – promotional launch
7 Public and press relations
8 Staff training
9 Training in managerial accounting and administration
10 Operational manuals
11 Training materials
12 A support team to launch the business
13 Financial arrangement with banks
14 Technical and legal backing

Operational manuals and training materials (videos, etc.) are of course tangible items, but most franchisors will wish to retain title rather than 'sell' the know-how of the business.

All of the above, including the costs of recruiting, can be costed, or a portion allocated based on sales projections and experience gained from the pilot operation. It should be appreciated that it will not be practical to recover all the costs, particularly in the early days of recruitment when acquisition costs tend to be high. However, the establishment of initial fees to a formula recognizing the various components will prove beneficial in ensuring all franchisees receive a soundly constructed launch programme.

Set-up costs

The franchisor will have incurred and will continue to incur set-up costs such as trade mark or service mark registration, contract costs, promotional literature and advertising for franchisees. It is unwise to endeavour to recover all of these by loading the initial fee. It is also unrealistic not to attempt to defray some of these expenses and allow a margin in the initial fee for contingencies and a contribution to these set-up costs.

As previously mentioned more and more franchisors are moving towards a management fee structure as the major source of ongoing revenue. As with initial fees there is no 'set' percentage for management or ongoing fees. Between franchise systems on offer in the UK fees vary from 2 per cent to 45 per cent of the franchisee's sales. There are numerous factors to take into account, the most important of these being:

Can the franchisee business afford the fee at all levels of sales?
Will the income from fees adequately compensate the franchisor?

The franchisor cannot expect to make a profit from the first few franchisees. It will cost as much to support the first three or four as the first twenty.

A fair return

It is relatively easy to identify what will be considered a fair return to the franchisee. Can this return be dramatically increased by additional support from the franchisor? What would be the cost of such support? Will the return to both parties justify this support? To charge too high a fee will more obviously harm the franchisee if he makes inadequate profits. To charge too low a fee will result in inadequate support and ultimately harm both parties.

It is obviously important to get the right balance and this can often be accomplished, as with the initial fee, by breaking it down into various components.

The ongoing fee is commonly the principal source of income to the franchisor from which to fund

1 support staff – whether in the field or at HQ
2 ongoing marketing, PR, sales
3 the franchisor's overheads
4 research and development
5 the franchisor's profit
6 ongoing training of franchisees and their staff

A key question for franchisors in identifying the level of support is 'What can I do for the franchisee that they cannot do for themselves?' Marketing, research and development are two obvious answers but others more specific to the individual franchise should be sought and considered. By analysing in this way the income necessary to provide the desired level of support plus a fair return to both parties, a fee can be established and tested through the pilot operations.

Promotional fee

The majority of franchisors, and subsequently franchisees, prefer to identify separately a marketing or promotional fee. Within the agreement there is usually a facility to conduct an audit to ensure that all the funds collected are used for the stated purpose. The benefits of this in an established franchise company are obvious but, when there are only a few franchisees, national or even regional promotion may be impractical and will certainly require a subsidy from the franchisor.

Arriving at the correct balance of fees is both an art and a science. The exercise should be gone through several times and financial advisers and banks consulted for their input. It is important not to be led too much by what other franchisors charge, but to consider the future more than the past and identify the ideal support needed now and the cost of development in the future.

It is essential to test continually the initial and ongoing formulae for the calculation of the fee, and to assess the effect changes have on the pilot operation (the potential franchisee's business) and the franchisor's business.

The offer

Having established the pilot operation and arrived at a suitable fee structure, the next stage is to develop the franchise package, that is, the offer that will be made to franchisees. It will contain all the elements necessary to set up the franchisee in his outlet or area with the optimum chance of success based on the franchisor's experience. It will include initial supplies; materials and equipment; training programmes; printed materials; promotional supplies; stock; and manuals covering operations, administration and sales, an identified area or site, financial models including profit and loss and cash flow projections, a financial package (probably arranged through one or more of the banks who offer arrangements for franchisees), reporting systems, ordering processes, etc.

The franchise package should be quantified and costed and a full list prepared under the following basic headings attached to a summary sheet. Typical headings would be as follows.

Franchise fee Includes training, training materials, and use of manuals covering marketing, administration and operation. Assistance in launch.

Promotional material Sales literature, menus, displays, wall cards, direct mail materials, signs.

Equipment List and price the items.

Shop/vehicle fittings Counters, tables, chairs, racking.

Stock Food, chemicals, etc.

The franchise contract is an important item in the franchise package. Indeed it brings together the terms and conditions of the franchise offer which the franchisor will make to prospective franchisees. Whilst franchise agreements usually have a basic form, it is important that a contract is drafted to meet the specific needs of the business and a specialist in such matters consulted.

In Appendix 1 we show the short-form franchise agreement by John Adams and K. V. Prichard Jones and in Appendix 2 the Kall-Kwik Printing (UK) Limited Franchise Agreement. It is not the intention to go through these contracts in detail but to comment on a few points of interest.

Both agreements commence by identifying the parties – Franchisor and Franchisee – and proceed to define some of the terms:

The Mark The name by which the franchisor is known and which the franchisee will be licensed to use.
The Know-how The systems and methods of the franchisor. In the case of Kall-Kwik these methods are derived from an American corporation – Kwik-Copy Corporation of Houston, Texas, USA.

Whilst the short-form contract gives space for a number of years from . . . to . . ., the Kall-Kwik contract is from commencement/ opening date until 8 October 2008. This is an unusual feature and may be a reference to the agreement Kall-Kwik have with the beneficial owner of the mark and know-how in America.

It is particularly interesting as this is a location franchise – that is, premises are an essential feature of the franchise. It is common in such franchises for the term of the lease and the agreement to match up as, obviously, the loss of premises part way through the term of the franchise agreement would pose a problem, as would the franchise agreement ending part way through the length of the lease.

Territories

The short-form agreement contains references to both location and territory, the latter being for use in mobile or area franchises. Defining a territory poses both an initial and an ongoing problem for the area franchisor. The pioneers of UK franchising, ServiceMaster and Dyno-Rod, both introduced new unique services where the demand in this country was unknown. To ensure the success of the franchisee, relatively large areas had to be allocated.

Those early single areas would, today, accommodate several outlets. As markets mature it is possible, through surveys of population, industry, socio-economic groupings, home ownership, etc., to assess more accurately the market potential of an area. However, there is no sure way of ensuring that a franchisee, or manager, will be effective in exploiting that potential.

Territorial rights are, probably, the greatest cause for concern amongst area franchisees and, as such, should be of concern to franchisors.

The franchisee, particularly the newcomer, will expect a degree of exclusivity or protection. It is extremely unlikely that a prospect would invest in a franchise if the understanding was that all the surrounding franchisees could do business in the area, yet, in an established franchise, they are almost certainly serving customers there now.

Paradox

New area franchisors are faced with a paradox. They obviously wish to meet customer needs, but to encourage franchisees to serve clients outside their allocated area will pose major problems when adjacent franchises are set up and the franchisor then wishes to discourage the very activity which was originally encouraged. One possible solution is to use a company-operated pilot operation to handle outside work. Territorial problems are likely to continue to arise and are not really resolved by lines on maps or exclusive agreements. Attempts to enforce exclusive areas may cause problems with the Restrictive Trade Practices Act 1976, although this may change in the near future if UK competition legislation relative to franchising falls in line with the block exemption for franchise agreements which was adopted by the Commission of the European Communities on 30 November 1988 and which was effective from 1 February 1989. Article 2 of the block exemption contains a clause restricting the right of the franchisee to solicit customers from outside his territory.

Both agreements identify separate promotional fees and separate accounts and controls so that franchisees can be sure the monies are spent for the benefit of the chain.

This brief look at one or two items will indicate the need for careful consideration and the advice of experienced advisers in drafting franchise agreements.

Recruiting franchisees

Whilst no method of selection of franchisees or staff can be considered foolproof, the process should be made as objective and administratively simple as possible. Failure to give attention to such detail can result in such fiascos as a driver being recruited with a heavily endorsed licence or designers who suffer from colour blindness!

By making the recruitment process more routine, as the organization grows and the responsibilities are delegated, the personal knowledge and insights of those who have previously done the job are not lost.

A franchisee role or job description is the starting point – this should outline the purpose, functions and responsibilities, communications, operating conditions and prospects linked to the job of being a franchisee. This leads to the next document – a franchisee specification – which specifies the kind of person best suited to the role and should be considered as the key document in the selection process. Such a specification can be based on two types of question. What attributes are *essential* in the prospective franchisee and what attributes would one *prefer*, i.e. the desirable attributes. The difference between the two should be clearly understood and is perhaps best illustrated by examples: good health and the ability to drive a motor vehicle will be essential to a mobile or van operated franchise; current involvement in some physical activity may be desirable, but would not disqualify a candidate who did not fulfil this requirement.

Biographical summary

A franchisee biographical summary form should be derived to gather both essential and other relevant information. This can be completed on the basis of an interview, allowing a rapport to be established whilst ensuring all the information required is obtained and recorded. An assessment form can also be a useful tool in identifying 'best' prospects and, when maintained over a period of time, will provide further insights into the characteristics which make for good or bad franchisees.

Identification and selection of franchisees in this manner provides a guide to the literature and recruitment package which will attract the right people and the most likely media in which to promote the franchise opportunity.

Just as the pilot operations will demonstrate success, so will the early success of the first franchises prove the concept and develop the image even more. A few highly successful well-supported franchises will provide a firm base for expansion.

Supporting franchisees

An essential feature of business format franchising is the continuing interest and concern a franchisor will have for the franchisee.

If the franchise is well constructed the growth of the franchisee will benefit the franchisor, the name will be better known and so both parties flourish. Providing the correct level of support requires careful planning. The new franchisor organization will inevitably be small but should contain specialists in the core business including operations, administration and marketing. Financial planning will have played an important role in the development of the pilot operation and a financial model specific to each franchisee will have been constructed as previously mentioned.

Individual franchisee performance should be compared with the model on a weekly or monthly basis and variances both positive and negative investigated promptly.

In a new dynamic business, organizational structure tends to evolve. Planning to restructure in line with the financial and human resources available will ensure that the needs of both the franchisee and franchisor continue to be met.

Franchisees invest in a franchised business not only to increase their prospects of success but also because they wish to belong. They expect regular contact, monitoring and control of both the qualitative and quantitative aspects of their business. It is not too surprising that the successful franchise systems tend to be the most structured and controlled.

A growing franchised business is likely to find a frequent need to restructure the organization. Functional specialists will always have a role in the core business but growth in the number of outlets may require field managers with motivational and interpersonal skills coupled with a general knowledge of the business.

As a franchisee's business grows, so too do the needs of that business. New skills may need to be taught as a result of growth or innovation. The franchisor will find a need to be continually involved in training both franchisees and their staff.

Protecting franchisees

The ongoing interest, both financial and personal, that franchisors have in their franchisees is a unique relationship often based on mutual trust and friendship. It can be immensely rewarding and extremely frustrating. Most franchisees have not been in business before and may have difficulty in handling large sums of money. It is the franchisor's responsibility to teach the franchisee all aspects of running a successful business including personal financial control.

The franchisor is responsible for understanding the market. From regular reports received from franchisees it should be possible to detect trends and movements in the market place and share these with the whole network of franchisees. More formal market research may be used as necessary.

A programme of research and development should be initiated to ensure technical competence in the face of economic and social changes and competitive threats.

This overall concern for franchisees will prove rewarding in both financial and human terms.

Summary

A model franchise company will

1 recruit, as franchisees, people who are qualified financially and by ability, energy and enthusiasm to make the most of the opportunity, and establish them in locations where there is an adequate market to meet the individual's financial and personal needs;
2 ensure complete and thorough training in all aspects of the business so that the franchisee has confidence in his ability to sell and produce, and to control his business;
3 maintain an ongoing interest in each franchisee through an effective two-way communication system, by monitoring performance and being sensitive to individual needs, to ensure potential is exploited and increasing profitability is the result;

4 ensure that an adequate supply of stock, materials, equipment, promotional and other necessary items are readily available;

5 provide ongoing training in all aspect of the business through one-to-one training, seminars, conferences and workshops;

6 have available advisers for consultation in marketing, finance, business administration and production techniques and ensure the increasing competence and professionalism of these and the organization as a whole;

7 be sensitive to

(a) changing market needs and segments,
(b) technical innovation and development,

and provide updated, revised or new programmes and systems to meet the same;

8 make representation on behalf of franchisees to groups, individuals, potential and existing customers and, in particular, concentrate on that market segment where the best results are to be obtained for the effort expended;

9 develop and maintain relationships and contacts with companies and organizations which can be beneficial to everyone in the network;

10 continually expand its distribution network and increase penetration of the market, and examine and develop new markets to spread the corporate name and provide new opportunities to both new and existing franchisees;

11 apply a proportion of its income towards the promotion and protection of the company's name, its methods and its systems;

12 grow increasingly profitable and ensure a strong financial base, increasing opportunities and the ability to continue to pursue excellence in all the above.

It can be seen from this chapter that the decision to become a franchisor is an important one which requires detailed planning and investigation from the initial business to the pilot operations, and beyond.

However, given that there is a proven business format, if the steps outlined above are followed, the franchisor will find that he is well equipped with the key tools for a successful franchising operation.

Key points

- Franchises should be properly planned.
- Pilot operations are essential.
- The franchise contract is a key document.
- There is no foolproof method of selecting franchisees.

6

The franchise relationship

Outline

This chapter looks at:

- the franchise contract
- the day-to-day reality of franchise independence
- franchisee associations

Introduction

Franchise offers a promising chemistry for combining the economies of scale enjoyed by the franchisor with the flexibility of the franchisee to exploit local market opportunities. But who is the typical franchisee, what are their backgrounds and motives in taking a franchise and how do such socio-economic factors influence the successful running of a franchise operation? Until recently, very little was known about such questions and the key to understanding the nerve centre of franchising – the franchise relationship – was shrouded in mystery and reliant, at best, upon anecdotal evidence. However, more recently, research has increased our knowledge in this area.

At one extreme, the franchisee's small business outlet can be viewed as an emerging form of independent small business, now common throughout most advanced industrial societies, whose main characteristic is its close association with another, usually larger, enterprise (the franchisor). This association, it could be said, is little different except in degree to that now found between many small businesses and other firms with whom they do business. Such a close association may be seen simply as a reflection of the fact that 'no firm is an island entire of itself' in a modern economy. Adopting a view at the opposite extreme, however, it might be argued that the franchised enterprise is, in reality, simply a *managed* outlet featuring in the corporate marketing strategy of another truly independent business – that of the franchisor.

In research conducted at the London Management Centre (involving over 400 franchisees and franchisors) to clarify this issue, the franchised small enterprise has been examined first in terms of its formal independence, that is, in terms of its contractual and legal aspects, and then in terms of the operational dimension. The latter concerns day-to-day relations. After all, all social and business relations develop a range of behaviours additional to those laid down in any contract. Real-life relations turn on a subtle balance of negotiations and either party may choose to ignore or depart from contractually prescribed patterns of conduct, possibly with the open or tacit approval, or at least the reluctant acceptance, of the other party to the transaction. In other words, the description of the formal level of association between franchisor and franchisee prompts the question: *What actually happens in practice?*

Formal independence

Information on the formal level of independence can be obtained through an analysis of franchise contracts. These tend to be characteristically detailed and comprehensive in specifying the nature of the relationship between franchisee and franchisor. In terms of franchisee independence, some of the provisions appear to restrict closely the franchisee's freedom of action as a businessman. One contract examined stipulated, for example, that the franchisee:

> Will conduct his franchised . . . business in all respects as shall be *laid down by the Company from time to time in the Manual or otherwise.* The franchisee will keep the copy of the Manual in his possession up to date with all variations thereto which the Company may make.

This form of contract has been extensively criticized by some American writers since it involves, in effect, the franchisee's commitment to an open-ended agreement. To quote one leading writer:

> Since the provisions of the operating manual can be changed at the prerogative of the franchisor, the franchisees find themselves in the

tenuous position of being bound to a contract that can be modified *unilaterally* by the franchisor.

Contracts are also often explicit in relation to restrictions on the franchisee's right to dispose of his franchised business. Sometimes the franchisor claims the right of first refusal to purchase and requires that written permission must be given before the outlet could be sold to another person. The franchisor also often insists on being informed of all the confidential details of any transaction – valuation of the premises, etc. – intended to result in the sale of an outlet. Some contracts have entitled the franchisor to around 10 per cent of the sale price of the franchise when it changes hands.

Of course, obligations are also imposed on the franchisor. But given that the contract is drawn up by the franchisor, it has the character of a *contract of adhesion* rather than a *contract of negotiation*. That is, rather than being the end result of a process of bargaining between parties, it is offered by one of the parties (the franchisor) on a take-it-or-leave-it basis. Franchisors are very reluctant to vary their standard contract to suit individual franchisees.

On the other hand, franchisors admit that they do sometimes vary certain aspects of the contract for a new franchisee particularly with regard to size of territory and, to a lesser extent, by modifying requirements on minimum capital required or other starting costs.

Over time, research shows that contracts are judged by franchisees to have become more comprehensive and more strictly enforced. Many franchisors report enforcement problems. Yet there are also indications that franchisors tend to tread lightly concerning contracts. For instance, franchisors do not report frequent mention of the contract in their relations with franchisees and over 80 per cent of those franchisees interviewed in the London Management Centre's research claimed that their franchisor *never* mentioned the contract to them in everyday relations.

Just over half of the above franchisees said that the contract favoured the franchisor, while almost 40 per cent thought it about neutral between the two parties. Only 6 per cent, on the other hand, felt that the contract was weighted in favour of franchisees. Despite these findings almost 60 per cent of franchisees stated that there was no particular section of the contract they felt should be altered. Although most franchisor respondents believed that they strictly enforced their contracts, franchisees – those over whom the contracts were allegedly being enforced – tended not to accept this view. Less than a quarter of franchisees reported feeling that the contract was 'very strictly' or 'fairly strictly' enforced.

In other words, at the formal level, relations between the franchisor and franchisee might be described as implicitly one-sided since the contract is drawn up on a virtually non-negotiable basis by the franchisor and put to the franchisee on a take-it-or-leave-it basis. But research findings also hint strongly that consideration of franchisor–franchisee relations solely at the formal level is misleading.

Interviews with both franchisors and franchisees suggest that the contract, although central in a formal sense to their relations, is not permitted a similarly explicit position in their day-to-day relations. For instance, franchisors not infrequently have to chase franchisees for monthly statements or royalty payments, but this rarely involves any explicit reference to the franchisee's contractual obligations. Instead, the appeal is usually framed in terms of the need for administrative efficiency and couched in the form of an informal, personal plea for co-operation from the franchisee.

Operational independence

The above discussion suggests that there is what might be termed an operational realm in franchisor–franchisee relations which is not necessarily revealed by an examination of contractual relations. It may be suggested that this is no less than might be expected given that no contract can fully define everyday relations and, more important, a contract of adhesion essentially embodies one party's view of how it would *like* relations to be patterned. In practice, all kinds of other influences will push and pull relations in other directions.

In the London Management Centre's research, franchisors and franchisees have been questioned on who they feel was responsible for certain key aspects of the outlet's operations. As exhibit 2 indicates, franchisors and franchisees tend to be in broad agreement on the division of responsibilities on seven key aspects of outlet decision making. Franchisors claim responsibility for control over the product/service mix and pricing while franchisees claim control

Operational element	Views	% franchisors agreeing with view (n = 15)	% franchisees agreeing with view (n = 215)
Additional deletions to product service	Mainly or totally the decision of the franchisor	93.3	55.3
Responsibility for pricing	Mainly or totally the decision of the franchisor	80.0	62.8
Hours of operation	Mainly or totally the decision of the franchisee	66.6[1]	78.1
Employment of staff/ staff wage levels	Mainly or totally the decision of the franchisee	60.0/ 93.3	93.5/ 88.4
Quality of service to the customer	Mainly or totally the decision of the franchisee	46.7	74.4
Bookkeeping	Mainly or totally the decision of the franchisee	73.3	85.1
Local advertising	Mainly or totally the decision of the franchisee	33.3[2]	91.6

[1]One franchisor claimed total responsibility for hours of operation which were precisely defined in the franchisor–franchisee contract.
[2]Eight of the 15 franchisors interviewed claimed that responsibility for local advertising was equally distributed between franchisor and franchisee.

Exhibit 2 Franchisor and franchisee views on control over operational elements of the franchised outlet

over hours of opening, employment of personnel, bookkeeping, service quality standards and local advertising.

However, these findings cannot be accepted as a total consensus of views. There are always sizeable minorities holding contrary views on some of these aspects and especially on quality control and product/service mix changes. Thus, some franchisees feel that they had equal say in product/service mix additions, deletions or alterations and somewhat surprisingly a minority even believed they have *most* influence.

Franchisor–franchisee communications

Another aspect of the franchisee's operational freedom was measured by day-to-day contact with the franchisor. Almost 35 per cent of franchisees interviewed in London Management Centre research reported contact with their franchisor as occurring at least once a week. For the remaining franchisees for whom information is available, the typical frequency of contact with their franchisor was once a month. Three-quarters reported that they, rather than the franchisor, initiated these contacts in the majority of instances. Their replies indicated that they were generally using the franchisor as a resource in these contacts, that is, seeking solutions to technical and other operating problems. In other words, a high proportion of franchisor–franchisee contacts were initiated by franchisees rather than by franchisors positively supervising franchisees.

Franchisees reported a relatively low level of franchisor representative visits to their outlets. Less than 10 per cent were visited more frequently than once a fortnight and 18 per cent claimed they were *never* visited. The typical reported frequency was monthly or bimonthly. These figures hardly betoken close supervision by franchisors and correlate well with franchisees' own preferences on the frequency of franchisor visits. They also correlate with the replies of franchisees of whom almost two-thirds felt that the level of assistance from their franchisor was about right. This did not mean that franchisees were uncritical of franchisors on the quality of assistance provided. Among those franchisees who had been operating their franchise for over a year, 17 per cent rated the assistance provided as 'poor' or 'very poor' while a further 34 per cent rated it as only 'adequate'. However, these findings have to be balanced against the almost 50 per cent who rated assistance provided by the franchisor as 'good' or 'very good'. Over time the level of approval tended to rise since most franchisees were more satisfied at the time of interview than they had been in their first six months of operation.

Assistance is not the same as supervision and franchisees were asked whether they would prefer more or less supervision from their franchisor. Only 5 per cent felt they were oversupervised while over 80 per cent felt the level was about right. Indeed, 12 per cent would have liked more supervision than they were currently receiving. Keeping in mind the adage that it is impossible to please all the people all the time, it does seem from these findings, and those in the preceding paragraphs, that franchisors have achieved a reasonable compromise between being perceived as providing too little assistance and oversupervising.

Control

Franchisors do encounter problems in maintaining what they feel is a satisfactory level of control over franchisees. Franchisors sometimes cite problems in getting franchisees to make proper and full financial returns on time and these problems sometimes tend to be greater with longer established franchisees. Marketing can also be a problem because all franchisors put great emphasis on this aspect but often felt that franchisees were very deficient in marketing skills. Most franchisors had instituted methods of detecting evasion in the form of incorrect financial information or franchisees purchasing supplies from non-approved sources. Finally, since maintaining the franchise's national image is crucial to its success, quality control at the outlet is a permanent problem – a single franchisee's failure here could do enormous damage to the franchise's reputation.

Commenting on the disadvantages of franchising from their point of view, it was the above issues that predominated in franchisor's replies. They conceded that *the franchise relationship inevitably meant a loss of control compared with the conventionally managed outlet*. It also required a more persuasive style of management, since franchisors were well aware that attempts to control franchisees too closely were likely to be counter-productive. This did not, of course, prevent them from exerting very close control over particular franchisees from time to time even to the point of terminating the contract if necessary but this was relatively rare.

Representation

Indications of possible tension in the operation realm from the franchisees' viewpoint are perhaps most clearly exemplified in the formation of franchisees' associations. The latter can take two forms. The first is the joint consultative committee set up by the franchisor for an exchange of views between franchisees and between franchisor and franchisees, over which the franchisor exerts sufficient control to ensure the association's activities broadly serve his interests. The second is an independent association freely founded and controlled by franchisees in a particular franchise with the aim of increasing their bargaining power *vis-à-vis* the franchisor and acting as a vehicle for exchanging ideas and information among franchisees. The first variety is often established to prevent the emergence of the second. Some franchisors freely expressed the view that the completely independent franchise association was too similar to a trade union, challenging franchisor authority and power.

Latent forces pushing franchisees into an independent association to protect their interests in relations with the franchisor are recognized on both sides of the franchising industry. Many franchisees support the idea of a national franchisee association. However, in relation to their own franchise, franchisees appear much less enthusiastic or even sceptical of what such an association might achieve. The response of franchisors whose franchisees have actually gone ahead and formed an independent association is usually that it is 'unnecessary' and causes 'hindrance and delays' in dealing with franchisees. Franchisee members, on the other hand, see such an association's main aim as serving their interests. Some franchisees believed the effect of such an association can be to achieve more favourable terms than would otherwise be the case.

New understanding

Recent research into franchising takes us forward from an earlier state of reliance upon anecdotes and hunches in our attempts at understanding some of the socio-economic processes involved in franchising. Perhaps not surprisingly, reality presents us with a rather more complex picture than existed previously.

One conclusion that can be drawn from research is that franchisees do not appear to differ greatly in terms of background and motivation from the conventional small business person. He/she comes from a similar background (though is often rather better educated) and often has earlier links with the world of self-employment. In fact, the actions of many who bought franchises were motivated by an interest in self-employment generally as much as franchising *per se*. Further, the differences between various franchises was quite substantial. That is, the capital requirements of entry had a substantial influence upon the kinds of people entering different franchises.

Franchising appears a good avenue into self-employment for certain kinds of people in particular. Amongst these are people whose previous employment in no way lends itself to self-employment. For instance, an ex-print-worker, garage mechanic or restaurant manager may well feel able to 'clone' a business they have previously worked for. However, someone coming out of the armed forces or a professionally trained production manager or designer from a large company may feel less well equipped to turn their previous experience into a business. None the less, they do have skills which can intertwine with those of a franchisor to build a complete business operation.

Many of the individuals participating in the London Management Centre's research had only been franchisees for a modest period of time: 2–5 years was typical. Given the rapid growth of franchising in recent years, this situation appears fairly common. The result of this is that there is little data available upon which to plot long-term trends in franchisee profitability. In addition, a strong reliance on borrowed finance in the early days plus marked variations in the initial capital requirements of the various franchises makes any assessment of success complex and difficult.

Views expressed by many franchisors tended to add weight to American research claims of a relationship between success as a franchisee and success in previous employment. However, all the franchisors were able to point to stark exceptions to this general rule.

On the question of the franchisor–franchisee relationship, at the operational level, the franchisee can enjoy fairly considerable independence. Franchisors might claim that, by virtue of the authority derived from the contract which forms the basis of the formal level of relations, franchisee prerogatives are strictly limited. On the other hand, franchisees are the only decision makers who, in practice, can effectively make certain decisions. Indeed, it might be doubted whether franchisors would ever *want* to make some of these decisions even if they then claimed the ultimate right to do so. For instance, one of the attractions of franchising for franchisors is *not* having to worry about personnel problems at the outlet level.

In other areas the franchisor's exercise of control is likely to be too remote or too late. Quality control over service to the customer at second hand, for example, is unlikely to be fully effective or when exercised is often an indication that things have already gone wrong. Typically, control is maintained through visits by the franchisor's field officers, but 'dummy' consumers may also be used or an open invitation made to dissatisfied customers on promotional literature or invoices to contact the franchisor's head office. However, as reported earlier, franchisor field representative visits may be infrequent and responding to consumer complaints means acting after the quality lapse has occurred.

More subtly, relations between franchisors and franchisees which relate to the latter's independence are also influenced by other latent factors. Franchisors need the goodwill of franchisees, and attempts to oversupervise or to impose new contractual obligations against the will of franchisees soon exhausts this goodwill. This may even promote an independent franchisee association thus increasing franchisee bargaining influence. Franchisors can cope with such an association but they usually prefer not to have to. There is also the threat of seeking external help to which franchisees could resort. For instance, politicians and the mass media offer further resources for franchisees. This is no idle threat for an industry which has shown itself to be very sensitive indeed towards its public image.

'Independence' is a relative notion and it is all too easy to discuss the degree of independence of the small franchised outlet on an implicit but misleading assumption that the conventional small business is unambiguously independent. Historically, the small enterprise, even when it was the typical or basic unit in the economy, operated under severe restrictions on its independence.

Many conventional small firms have much larger firms as their main customers and this may also constitute a severe limitation on independence without affecting the nominal or legal definition of independence. In Britain, for instance, one well-known high street chain store has become notorious for gradually strengthening links between itself and a host of small suppliers to the point where the latter are almost totally dependent on what has become the main buyer of their product. The buyer stipulates product design and quality, delivery and price and the small supplier is strongly discouraged from seeking other customers. The Bolton Report, in Britain, estimated that, in the manufacturing industry, 35 per cent of small firms were dependent on one customer for 25 per cent or more of their business. A similar picture emerges from other economies.

Many conventional small enterprises *are* much more independent than the typical franchised outlet but the difference remains a *relative* one. In other words, rather than a dichotomy we may suggest a continuum of independence with various kinds of small enterprise being located on different points of the continuum. A priori, we need not assume that franchised small businesses are necessarily always located at the least independent end of the continuum.

Key points

- There is more to franchising than just the contract.
- Franchises can vary very considerably from one to another.
- Franchisees in the *same* franchise sometimes report very different experiences.

7
Working out if franchising is right for you

Outline

This chapter looks at:

- how to assess your own motivation
- knowing yourself
- knowing your franchise

Introduction

In many ways the most difficult assessment you are required to make when thinking of becoming a franchisee is an assessment of yourself. In attempting to make such an assessment, you may find it worthwhile to canvass the views of others close to you who you feel can be objective. Any such assessment needs to cover four main issues: your motivation, personal resources, interests and personal characteristics.

Many people in business claim that their prime motivation is not money. In fact, many might earn more elsewhere, especially considering the effort and risks involved. That is not to say that some businessmen or women do not make very good profits but, for most, a *reasonable* rather than *flamboyant* lifestyle is what can be expected. Many of the main rewards to be gained are what might be termed *intrinsic* rewards. That is, they concern the nature of the activity and the emotional sense of involvement and personal satisfaction. Typical here are the following:

Independence and autonomy The satisfaction gained from structuring one's own time and efforts (within limits) rather than being directly supervised and controlled by others.

Finding an outlet for personal abilities   Many jobs in employment confine the individual to working on a narrow range of tasks. Thus, the work becomes repetitive and relatively unchallenging. In your own business you are responsible for a wide range of functions and activities – it can prove stressful and demanding but seldom boring.

Being able to pick the people you work with   Within certain limits (such as who you can afford to employ, who is available, etc.) you can select the people you work with rather than being at the mercy of an employer who picks them for you.

The status of being your own boss   No one is ever completely their own boss (you still have to meet the demands of customers, suppliers, bankers, etc.) but, none the less, having your own firm is as close as most people can aspire to this in a modern society and the role of self-employed businessmen is one enjoying considerable status and prestige.

Social satisfactions   This stems from an identification with all aspects of the product or service your business is involved in. Social contacts with the wide range of people and institutions linking with your business (right through from supplier to final customer) offer more interest and variety than is normal in employment.

In summary, the above satisfactions tend to be the ones that are most readily attained by working for oneself. For anyone considering going it alone but seeking very different goals and having very different motivations, setting up a business may not be the best route.

Personal characteristics or capacities are often of paramount importance in determining the success of a business venture. Running a business is a way of life rather than a mere job. It requires a fairly obsessive temperament and a capacity for dealing with stress.

Who becomes a successful franchisee?

The question of what sort of person is most likely to become a successful franchisee is one which, quite rightly, exercises the minds of both franchisor and potential franchisee. The remainder of this chapter is written with both in mind since there are obvious advantages to each in understanding the other party's position.

In primitive societies, personal characteristics, such as physical strength, tend to assume great importance in deciding the order of things. In advanced societies, such as our own, we like to think that we have moved on from there. But just how far are we able to identify the demands of a particular role, such as that of the franchisee, and select people who are the most likely to fulfil them successfully?

One everyday example of this question of selection indicates that we should err on the side of caution before thinking we have the problem licked. When trying to find marriage partners, we chalk up a surprisingly high official failure rate of one in three and in that case we are not just basing our judgement on an interview and a couple of bank references – we devote literally months, or even years, to it!

Let us look at a number of statements plucked from articles and brochures on franchising which quite clearly spell out the great importance of franchisee selection.

- 'Franchising is a partnership. A franchise's major asset, once established, is its franchisees.'
- 'A model franchise company will recruit as franchisees people who are not only qualified financially, but also by ability, energy and enthusiasm to make the most of the opportunity available to them.'
- 'Setting up a franchise is less difficult than managing it later on – you have to live with your earlier mistakes and a lot of those are people you pick when the urge for rapid growth takes over from all other considerations.'

Picking winners

Picking winners is *not* a simple task and the difficulties inherent in the situation tend to be compounded by a number of additional factors:

- Most developing franchises have much in common with the typical small firm in that they only have a few key staff members

79

undertaking a multitude of tasks. Most of these are very able and committed people but, usually, none of them is expert in the field of personnel management which is the relevant specialism here.

- Some franchisors may feel that they can rely on 'instinctive' or 'gut' feelings to signal good or bad franchisee prospects. Just as few people would admit to being a bad driver, so they feel it reflects badly on them if they admit to difficulties in selecting personnel.

- Very often people fall into the trap of looking for others *exactly like themselves*, when what they may well be best advised to do is look for people who complement rather than duplicate their own abilities. After all, no football team would get far with all defenders, or all forwards.

- Inasmuch as franchising is a team effort, one of the key frontline teams is the franchisee husband/wife. If these teams are not operating effectively, then a source of potential strength can descend into a weakness.

Conversion ratio

Research recently conducted shows that most of the more professional franchise companies convert no more than 4 per cent of initial enquiries for franchise prospectuses into sales. Even this is judged by some to be, if anything, on the high side, with 2 per cent being a better target figure. But why should it be so low?

One reason is that self-employment is a pipe-dream for quite a large army of people, who like to indulge in half-way-house experiences. They subscribe to magazines, attend seminars, visit exhibitions, join business clubs, and, in this way, get an arm's-length thrill of 'a share of the action'.

Some of these people may, eventually, take the plunge, should they lose their job, or come into some money, etc. But, for the meantime, they are not serious prospects.

Another reason is that self-employment is a widely held desire in our society, albeit that it is often combined with very little knowledge of what is involved. Grand notions abound of independence – 'doing your own thing', 'no one looking over your shoulder', 'play a round of golf on a midweek afternoon when the course is empty'.

Finance is often thought to be no great problem since the clearing banks exist for precisely that purpose. However, many people have never previously raised business loans, or any other loans for that matter, and the idea of having to offer security or collateral can come to them as a surprise.

Psychologists

Some psychologists have made an industry of attempting to devise tests which will predict those likely to make a success of self-employment and those who are unlikely to do so.

Whilst success to date in this field has been limited, it is perhaps worth mentioning a couple of the more hopeful approaches.

Probably, the best known is associated with Professor McClelland and attempts to measure 'need-achievement', or 'the desire to do well for the sake of an inner feeling of personal accomplishment'. In the 1960s this was used in many countries for selection and training purposes but, after some initial successes, it has come in for increasing criticism.

Another psychological test is the so-called 'locus of control' which is based on the proposition that potential successful entrepreneurs have a 'high internal locus of control' or, in other words, believe that they control their own behaviour and that their behaviour determines what happens to them. Again, there have been some successes claimed, but locus of control testing is still not widespread in the field of entrepreneurial selection

There appears to be a common misconception among franchisors that franchisees are very different animals from conventional independent small businessmen. However, research shows this is not the case. Often, when franchisors talk of 'entrepreneurs' they are thinking of the Freddie Lakers and Clive Sinclairs of this world, rather than the typical small businessman with whom their contact may have been limited.

Some guidelines for the franchisor

Some franchise companies may wish to explore the possible advantages of psychological profiling in depth. If they do, they would be well advised to seek specialist help. Short of this, what do the lessons of research and management theory generally hold to assist the franchisor in improving franchisee selection methods?

In a nutshell, they offer three messages for the franchisor.

• Carry out some research to see what sort of backgrounds franchisees typically come from. For instance, if 100 people apply for your prospectus, what does research tell us is the *single* best indication as to who are the two or three most likely seriously to follow through and become franchisees? Answer: there is a history of previous self-employment in the family (see chapter 4).

Two major research studies in Britain, and one in the US show that, overall, something like one in three of people who become franchisees have some previous history of self-employment. Moreover, one in two have been either self-employed themselves, or have a parent with experience of self-employment. This separates them out very distinctively from the population at large.

• Make use of standard personnel techniques to ensure that your interview and selection/counselling procedures are as scientific as possible and protect you against subjective or whimsical judgements. For instance, you should develop a proper licensee role description. This should outline the purpose, functions, responsibilities, conditions and prospects linked to the role.

Then, you should have a licensee specification which should outline the kind of person best suited to the role and provide the *key* document in the selection process. Put simply, this document is based on the answers to two questions: which attributes are *desirable* in the franchisee, and which are *essential*. Thereafter biographical summary and assessment procedures are needed.

• In addition to the above, you can generate your own franchisee diagnostic questionnaire schedule, suited to your own franchise operation (see below).

Whilst it remains true that there is no single foolproof formula, or litmus paper test, that will guarantee the franchisor a 100 per cent success rate in franchisee selection, careful thought and consideration should, at the very least, improve selection by a worthwhile margin and by doing so bring about long-term benefits for both the franchise network and its franchisees.

The diagnostic questionnaire

The diagnostic questionnaire is a tool designed by Professor John Stanworth of the London Management Centre at the Polytechnic of Central London to fit into the franchise company's battery of personnel techniques. Alternatively, it can be adopted for independent use by potential franchisees.

The diagnostic questionnaire itself takes the form of a series of questions and operates on a 'forced choice' principle. That is, each question offers a choice of three responses: (a), (b) and (c). The prospective franchisee is asked, under each question, to select the statement which he/she feels most accurately describes them. They should opt for one of the responses to the exclusion of the others. This is a device to stop people sitting on the fence. It is quick and simple to administer and also gives leads on issues that can be followed up in more detail later.

When is it used?

The timing of its use by franchisors can be organized to suit the needs of individual companies but the possibilities are numerous:

- It can be sent out with the company's initial information pack as part of a first response to enquiries. This can have the advantage of making prospects think through their own position and spelling out some of the issues involved in being a franchisee. This initial educational function can be valuable in 'cooling out' some of the 'dreamers'. Franchisors might even suggest that potential franchisees not only complete the exercise for themselves but also get someone else to complete it for them as an aid to checking out the image others have of them.
- Its use can be delayed until, say, the first interview stage when the franchisor has the choice of allowing the prospective franchisee to

complete it in private unaided, or with the franchisor administering it as part of a face-to-face interview.

- It can be used when discussions are well advanced and then used to the advantage of both parties as an additional check of their understanding of each other.

Which of the above alternatives is preferable depends on the franchisor's other selection/recruitment techniques but, on balance, the first probably has most to offer since it makes the prospective franchisee think through his/her situation as well as providing the franchisor with valuable information.

Interpreting replies

There is a marking scheme for interpreting the replies in terms of whether or not they are favourable to the requirements of your particular franchise or not. Thus, for each of the 20 questions below, three statements attract two, one or zero marks respectively. If you wish to use this exercise principally to inform the prospect of what is involved in franchising and whether they are likely to be suitable material, you may provide them with the marking scheme to facilitate *self-assessment* and, in the process, allow them to see which statements are regarded favourably by you in terms of relevance to your franchise.

On the other hand, if the main reason for running the exercise is to get information from the potential franchisee in as accurate a form as possible, the franchisor may mark the completed questionnaire himself. If the prospect does not know which statements carry most marks, he/she is less likely to be tempted to select the statements attracting most points. It is worth stressing the point that giving dishonest answers in order merely to accumulate points is a fruitless exercise from all points of view.

Obviously, any company using this technique can add to the questions below or may wish to drop some or reallocate the points on certain questions. For instance, some companies are looking for franchisees who are very ambitious and wish to grow. Others selling what may be called 'job franchises' better suited to a one-person operation may feel that such ambition could be stifled or counter-productive. Many franchisors express a preference for people coming from *outside* the line of business in question. Others, however, may see advantages in recruiting people from similar lines of business. Changing the points scheme to accommodate such in-house preferences is a relatively simple matter.

Questions

Twenty suggested questions are listed below accompanied by a marking scheme presented in angular brackets, thus ⟨ ⟩. A short explanation of the issues and implications of each question follows further on.

Question 1 Are you regarded by those who know you as:

(a) Generally a fairly self-contained person? ⟨2⟩
(b) Generally a rather gregarious person? ⟨0⟩
(c) Somewhere in between (a) and (b)? ⟨1⟩

Question 2 Are you regarded by those who know you as:

(a) Frequently frustrated by tasks you find boring? ⟨0⟩
(b) Able to endure a reasonable amount of boredom and frustration? ⟨1⟩
(c) Generally good at concentrating on whatever tasks face you? ⟨2⟩

Question 3 Would you say that:

(a) You possess an excess of mental and physical stamina and enjoy excellent health? ⟨2⟩
(b) You find that you tire easily if you try to work long hours and your health is not always of the best? ⟨0⟩
(c) You estimate that your health and stamina are about average for a person of your age? ⟨1⟩

Question 4 Would you say that:

(a) You find mistakes and setbacks very demoralizing? ⟨0⟩
(b) You feel that mistakes can be a very useful way of learning as long as they are not repeated? ⟨2⟩
(c) You try to learn from your mistakes but often find it easier said than done? ⟨1⟩

85

Question 5   Which of the following most accurately describes you?

(a) You set yourself targets and almost obsessively chase after them?   (2)
(b) You get fed up if you find yourself 'on the go' all the time?   (1)
(c) You like to take life at a modest pace and respond to pressures as and when they arise?   (0)

Question 6   Would you say that:

(a) You find it almost impossible to make tough decisions, particularly if they involve people?   (0)
(b) You can make tough decisions when necessary but the process takes a lot out of you emotionally?   (1)
(c) You see tough decisions as a fact of life – you don't necessarily enjoy them but, on occasions, see no alternative?   (2)

Question 7   Would you say that:

(a) You do not suffer fools gladly and make little attempt to hide your feelings?   (0)
(b) You have notable patience and self-control?   (2)
(c) You are situated in between positions (a) and (b)?   (1)

Question 8   Would you say that:

(a) Your mood is very influenced by events?   (0)
(b) Your mood is very little influenced by events?   (1)
(c) You tend to adopt a policy of 'taking the rough with the smooth'?   (2)

Question 9   Are you regarded by people who know you as:

(a) A person who needs to know exactly where they stand?   (0)
(b) A person who can live with uncertainty?   (2)
(c) A person who can endure a reasonable amount of uncertainty?   (1)

Question 10   If you go into business would you:

(a) Resent people who appeared to be trying to tell you how to run your own business?   (0)

(b) Regard the views of others as a potential source of useful information and guidance? (2)

(c) Be willing to listen to others when you had the time but likely to 'take it all with a pinch of salt'? (1)

Question 11 Would you say that your total personal assets and savings together:

(a) Exceed the full buy-in cost of the franchise? (2)
(b) Exceed two-thirds of the full buy-in cost? (1)
(c) Amount to less than two-thirds of the full buy-in cost? (0)

Question 12 Do you feel that your spouse:

(a) Feels that how you earn a living is very much your own affair? (0)
(b) Would prefer to see you doing something you enjoyed? (1)
(c) Is very keen on your taking a franchise and willing to back you very strongly? (2)

Question 13 Which of the following is true of you?

(a) There is no history of self-employment in your family involving either yourself or close relatives (0)
(b) Though you have not personally been self-employed previously, there is some history of self-employment in your family via close family and/or relatives (1)
(c) You have personally been self-employed previously (2)

Question 14 Is your main reason for wanting to be a franchisee:

(a) To achieve a good standard of living? (2)
(b) Because most of the alternative options for making a living appear closed? (0)
(c) For the independence and autonomy involved in having your own business? (1)

Question 15 Do you feel that, in taking a franchise:

(a) You would have a tried and tested product/service which should 'sell itself'? (0)

(b) No matter how good the product/service, customers still respond to sales effort? (1)

(c) Selling would still be a key activity? (2)

Question 16 Is your prior work experience:

(a) Unrelated to the franchise in question? (2)

(b) Very closely related to the franchise in question? (0)

(c) Marginally related to the franchise in question? (1)

Question 17 In running your own business, would you:

(a) Prefer to stay small? (0)

(b) Wish to grow as much as circumstances allowed? (2)

(c) Grow to a size where you could begin to take more time out of the business? (1)

Question 18 Do you feel that:

(a) To get a job done properly, you must do it yourself? (0)

(b) Delegation allows you to spend your time doing what you are best at? (2)

(c) Delegation is a necessary evil? (1)

Question 19 Do you usually feel that it pays to:

(a) Take a long-term view of things? (2)

(b) Make hay whilst the sun shines? (0)

(c) Adopt a medium-term view? (1)

Question 20 Do you feel that:

(a) Your future lies largely in your own hands? (2)

(b) You can at least influence your own future? (1)

(c) The individual is merely a puppet on the end of a string and can do little to influence events? (0)

Issues

The issues being examined above are basically examining the ability to:

Q1 cope with the isolation of self-employment
Q2 exercise self-discipline
Q3 work long hours under pressure
Q4 learn from failure
Q5 compete with self-imposed standards
Q6 take unpopular decisions
Q7 resist impetuous or emotional behaviour
Q8 take a balanced view of events
Q9 tolerate uncertainty
Q10 accept advice
Q11 demonstrate financial viability
Q12 demonstrate support of spouse
Q13 demonstrate enterprise background
Q14 demonstrate profit motivation
Q15 demonstrate sales orientation
Q16 demonstrate receptiveness towards franchisor's training
Q17 demonstrate growth orientation
Q18 demonstrate a favourable attitude towards task delegation
Q19 take the long-term view
Q20 demonstrate belief that individuals can 'make things happen'.

The marking scheme, contained in the body of the questionnaire and presented in angular brackets ⟨⟩ should, in practice, be separated out. If a franchisor does *not* wish a prospective franchisee to be able to conduct his/her own marking, this should be withdrawn totally. A good score for the exercise in its present form would be in the 20–30 range. On a final note, no exercise like this can ever be *totally* efficient in predicting success. It is essential that it is used in association with other personnel techniques. With that proviso, it should pay good dividends.

Further detail

To add more 'meat to the bone' here, what follows is a more detailed outline of the issues involved in the one-liner question issues raised above:

Q1 Ability to cope with feelings of isolation – in contrast to being an employee, you have no boss, or other people in the same organization doing the same job, who can give help, advice and moral support. To put it more precisely, it is usually of little concern to anyone else whether you succeed or fail.

Q2 Ability to exercise self-discipline – in running your own business, you are responsible for a wide range of tasks. Some of these you will almost certainly find satisfying whilst others will prove highly frustrating.

There is no one but yourself responsible for allocating your time and you can, at your peril, neglect tasks such as paperwork, financial control, invoicing and chasing payment. Although these tasks may appear to be stopping you from getting on with the 'real job' of producing and selling, no business can survive without them.

Q3 Ability to work long hours under pressure – in running your own business, you are seldom off duty. Thus you require both mental and physical stamina. In the early days of a new business, there is little time for leisure activities, holidays or illness. Some advisers go as far as to recommend that anyone setting up a new business should consult their doctor first.

Q4 Ability to learn from failure – disappointments are inevitable in business and can lead to demoralization. A good businessman, however, must possess the resilience to survive set-backs and learn from them.

Q5 Ability to compete with self-imposed standards – when working for yourself, targets and standards need to be set which act as goals reinforcing motivation. If these goals are set too low they have little motivating force. If they are set unrealistically high, they will not be achieved and a sense of failure and demoralization may result. Thus, modestly ambitious, though not unrealistic, goals need to be set and used as markers of achievement.

Q6 Ability to take unpopular decisions – it is impossible to remain popular at all times and any attempt to do so is likely to have costly consequences for your business.

Q7 Ability to resist impetuous or emotional behaviour – in the face of frustration, it is tempting to react in what might later be seen as a whimsical manner that is not in the longer-term interests of the business. This may be emotionally satisfying in the short term but should be resisted at all costs – emotions must be kept under control.

Q8 Ability to take a balanced view of events – it is easy to yield to the temptation of feelings of euphoria or depression in response to good or bad news. This can prove extremely stressful and wearing. A successful businessman needs to be able at all times, to take a balanced view of events, to take 'the rough with the smooth'.

Q9 Ability to tolerate uncertainty – in an environment dominated by large organizations, the setting up of a new business is a highly creative venture and requires a facility for surviving uncertainty. People with a low tolerance of uncertainty experience difficulties in coping with the resulting stress.

Q10 Ability to take outside advice – having gone into business to gain a certain level of independence, it often requires a determined effort to be able to seek out and act on external advice but, again, this capacity needs to be exercised.

Q11 Ability to demonstrate financial viability – though the clearing banks tend to lend to would-be franchisees more readily than to would-be conventional small business start-ups, it needs to be remembered that all loans have to be repaid, with interest. A large financial repayment overhead in the early days of trading can impose additional pressures.

Q12 Ability to demonstrate support of spouse – most franchise outlets involve long hours of working and domestic disruption. In a large proportion of cases, there is some advantage to the spouse actually working in the running and/or administration of the business. Thus, anything less than positive support can have very negative consequences.

Q13 Ability to demonstrate enterprise background – despite the desire for self-employment being quite common, relatively few make the leap from aspiration to reality. Those who have previous direct experience of self-employment or, alternatively, have had a close relative self-employed (usually a father) appear to find the transition easier. Some evidence exists to suggest that they may also be more successful as measured in terms of business growth.

Q14 Ability to demonstrate profit motivation – amongst small business people generally, the desire for growth is of a rather low order and profit motivation is of a lower order than other goals such as independence and autonomy. Most small businesses, in fact, never employ anyone other than the owner.

In the case of a franchise, however, the pressures to push for growth of profits and size of business are usually quite strong.

Q15 Ability to demonstrate sales orientation – despite national advertising and the promotion of brand awareness by the franchisor, sales skills on the part of the franchisor can still make a very substantial difference to levels of market penetration. Local advertising and good interpersonal skills and service at the customer interface can be crucial.

Q16 Ability to demonstrate receptiveness towards the franchisor's training – franchisors tend towards the view that 'starting with a clean sheet' is the best basis for a training programme rather than competing with, or attempting to displace, previous training that a potential franchisee may have already had in the field concerned.

Q17 Ability to demonstrate growth orientation – the income of the franchisor is directly related to the growth of franchisees. Thus, franchisees easily satisfied with low levels of growth may require considerable motivating.

Q18 Ability to delegate – one serious growth constraint on most small businesses is the lack of willingness or ability to delegate.

Q19 Ability to take a long-term view – in an economy suffering from endemic 'short-termism', long-term planning and goal setting is likely to pay dividends.

Q20 Ability to 'make things happen' – people with an 'internal locus of control' tend to believe that they personally can influence their environment. This belief can become a self-fulfilling prophecy.

Key points

- It is important to know yourself as others know you.
- Franchising and self-employment do not suit many – be realistic!
- Don't take a franchise just as a last resort.

8

Overview and conclusions

For many individuals and many businesses, franchising has worked successfully. However, as is inevitable in business, there have been casualties and there will be more in the future. Franchising is no panacea or route to easy profits for either franchisee or franchisor.

Although the pyramid selling operations which gave franchising such a bad image some years ago have now departed, potential franchisees will need to continue to be cautious, since no legal framework can be totally comprehensive and other unscrupulous operators will continue to visit the world of franchising from time to time. These can often be recognized simply by the unlikely nature of the claims they make. Offers of 'success beyond your wildest dreams' are invariably just that – dreams.

However, some high-risk ventures in franchising operate from sound and respectable motives. Some take the form of new businesses that are attempting to franchise prior to being properly market tested and proven. Others are large companies in competitive markets hoping to shed overheads and supervisory costs by franchising without shedding very much in the way of profits. The problem here is usually undue optimism and unrealistic expectations rather than any deliberate intention to mislead potential investors.

Failure rates

One of the hottest debates in the field of franchising over the years has been the true level of franchise failure rates. The argument is that failure rates amongst franchised businesses are 'vastly' lower than those for conventional independent businesses. However, many of the people who write in this area, in truth, understand little about the specialist field of assessing business failure rates.

On the issue of franchise failure rates, there are a number of points that need to be kept in mind. Firstly, there are good reasons why a franchised business outlet *should* stand a better chance of success than a conventional one, particularly at the start-up stage. After all, what is a franchisee buying into if not a tried and tested business format?

Conventional small businesses, on the other hand, are very vulnerable in their early days. Many people who set up on their own do so in a haphazard manner with a minimum of planning. Their basic business idea may be flawed, sales projections may be hopelessly over-optimistic, the business may be under-capitalized from the outset, financial control mechanisms may be non-existent, etc.

When a person buys into a franchise, on the other hand, there should have been some assessment of their suitability to run a business *per se* and they should know the capital requirements needed to become successfully established. If you cannot raise sufficient funding, you should not be allowed across the starting line.

That is the theory and much of the time that is how things turn out. None the less, myths concerning success rates continue to survive and often enjoy the status of industry 'folklore'. Most of the people who write on this issue present figures which are highly dubious and, most worrying of all, they are usually unaware of either the origins or the inaccuracy of the figures they use.

The publisher's press release which accompanied the publication of one book on franchising recently said: 'It is reckoned that as many as 90 per cent of all new businesses fail whereas 90 per cent of new franchises succeed.' The origin of claims such as these appears to be a publication by the International Franchise Association (IFA) entitled *Franchising the Odds-On Favourite* which claimed that: 'Even if the actual franchise failure rate were eight times greater than reported, it would still pay an investor to be franchised rather than start an independent small business.'

The IFA admitted that their figures excluded 'illegitimate fringe' activities surrounding the field of franchising which would have altered the picture somewhat. But, even so, errors in their researchers' methodology and interpretation of official statistics on conventional small businesses were so gross as to attract the attention of academic researchers of some note, working for the American Small Business Administration (SBA), which was itself involved in funding individual entry into franchising at that time.

The SBA was able to induce the IFA to act in accordance with their researchers' recommendation that:

> The International Franchise Association withdraw from circulation all copies of the book *Franchising the Odds-On Favourite* . . . The book presents grossly inaccurate data on failure rates and would be very misleading to potential franchisees.

None the less, these figures entered the public arena with greater force than their withdrawal. They, and figures like them, continue to circulate and potentially mislead. The most accurate and honest statement that can be made on the issue of comparative failure rates is that made by Janet Housden in her own book on franchising in 1984 where she said:

> It has been claimed that as well as helping in the creation of new businesses, franchising substantially reduces the subsequent rate of failure in such businesses . . . No firm evidence has yet been produced to support this contention, but it seems reasonable to assume that franchised outlets of a reputable system are less likely to fail than independently-owned outlets, because of the franchisor's vested interest.

Our knowledge in this field is advancing slowly. The researchers (above) who were working for the SBA in the early 1970s, conducted an in-depth study of American fast-food franchising and estimated that, during the two-year period 1969–70, the failure rate was somewhere between 6.7 and 20.1 per cent of all fast-food *franchise systems* (franchisors). *Franchisee* failure rates were about one-third that level.

Lest these statistics appear confusing, although the rate of franchise system failure was quite high, many of the failures occurred amongst smaller systems with relatively few franchisees.

The problems with calculating failure rates are many. The key ones, however, are poor response rates to research questionnaires; the fact that 'ethical' franchisors are more likely to reply than 'unethical' ones; systems that have failed and disappeared are unlikely to reply; and it is difficult to distinguish between *turnover* rates and *failure* rates. If a franchise system is doing badly, franchisees may sell out to other investors due to low profit (or loss) figures but outlets continue in existence and may not register as individual franchisee failures.

Recent advances in methods of calculating survival rates amongst conventional small businesses indicate that these are probably rather higher than had previously been imagined – about 40 out of every 100 new firms probably survive the first ten years (this will vary somewhat with the business sector involved). Also, if we look at the British Franchise Association's own figures for 1986 (again based on very low response rate research), and if we aggregate outlet closures and those changing hands, we get a figure for the year of around 10 per cent.

Failure rates amongst well-tried and tested franchises are almost certainly lower than amongst conventional small businesses, but the relative balance is almost certainly not as big as is frequently claimed. Also, it should be remembered that, whilst franchisees may enjoy the benefits of the corporate strength of their franchisor while it lasts, we live in an age of change. Companies fail, some are bought and sold and others experience substantial turbulence from within. Within recent times, a founder-member company of the BFA changed hands and around two-thirds of the franchisees felt strongly enough about the resulting changes to leave their new franchisor.

The future of franchising

The current rapid rate of growth of franchising in Britain, and indeed internationally, appears set to continue. However, it is unlikely that the future will simply produce more of the same. With a rapidly changing economy and the notion of a single world market (global village) becoming ever more a reality, some intrinsic aspects of the nature of franchising itself are bound to change.

One key factor encouraging the growth of franchising is the world-wide decline of traditional manufacturing industry and its replacement by service sector activities. Franchising is especially well suited to service and labour-intensive activities, particularly when these require a large number of geographically dispersed outlets serving local markets.

One of the fastest growing sectors in the entire economy is that of business services and this itself is at least partly linked to the tendency of larger firms to buy in services which they previously ran in-house. In the future, the desire for greater flexibility and reduced overheads, which has spawned a boom in sub-contracting, will increasingly act as a factor promoting growth in franchising.

In the US, the business services sector grew from around 2 per cent of franchise outlets in 1970 to over 10 per cent by the mid 1980s. The sector includes activities such as employment agencies, printing services, accounting, credit and collection agencies, real estate, security, computing, marketing and market research, fund raising, etc.

These services are delivered by small franchised outlets and their clients include both large firms, who do not wish to produce such services under their own roof, and many small to medium-sized firms. This market, along with the growing demand for health, fitness and leisure-oriented services would promise substantial growth in the run up to the year 2000.

A further factor working in favour of the growth of franchising is the growth in popularity of self-employment generally. Most governments in the Western world are looking towards self-employment and small business as an important source of future jobs and, in Britain over the last decade, the proportion of the labour force in self-employment has increased from 7 to 12 per cent. As franchising becomes increasingly well known and understood, it is likely that it will appeal to a growing number of people.

The increased use of information technology by large organizations is resulting in ever-tighter managerial control systems and the gradual erosion of the independence and discretion from many white-collar jobs. This will be an additional factor leading to the search by middle class groups for more control over their own destiny.

International movements towards the harmonization of commercial legislation (the European Single Market for instance) and the development of legislation granting franchise activities exemption from certain laws of competition, all help to pave the way for a further substantial expansion of franchising. Of particular interest here, in a European context, was the announcement by the European Community of a 'block exemption' for franchise agreements from competition rules embodied in Articles 85 and 86 of the Treaty of Rome.

These had previously challenged various elements of franchise agreements: for example, on restrictions attached to purchases of supplies and equipment, the definition of specific franchise territories with boundary limitations, obligations to preserve secrecy before and after the termination of an agreement and, finally, obligations not to be involved in a competitive company.

Between now and the year 2000, an increasing proportion of the British economy is likely to come under foreign influence and control. Looking at the economy as a whole, Japan is likely to have the greatest single influence. However, if we restrict our interest to franchising, then America will probably be the key power. Already there are over 350 American business format franchisors operating over 30,000 outlets covering most countries of the world. Moving between countries is often facilitated by the master licensee system whereby a single individual or company receives the right to develop a franchise system throughout a specific country or region.

The heaviest concentrations of American franchises at present are in Canada, Japan, Continental Europe and the United Kingdom respectively. With the decentralization of the Socialist economies of Eastern Europe, further opportunities for crossing economic barriers are likely there.

The continued growth of franchising is all very well for the franchisor but what of the franchisee? The position of the franchisee has been hotly contested for many years. Even back in the 1960s, some people were urging tighter franchise regulations to protect franchisees (and potential franchisees) and were urging the industry to 'abandon the myth' that a franchise holder is an independent businessman.

However, research in Britain has shown that franchising, at its best, can represent a genuine partnership of interests and that franchisees can enjoy quite high degrees of independence. However, certain factors may act to reduce this over the next decade.

First is the possible tendency for contracts to become more detailed, directive and strictly enforced. Recently German and Danish courts have deemed particular franchise contracts to be so tight as to bestow employee status upon their holders. As franchisors become increasingly skilled in running franchise operations, there will be strong temptations to inject higher and higher levels of control into relationships with franchisees. Developments in the field of information technology, which are leading to tighter controls in a wide range of other jobs, may accentuate trends here.

Another factor changing the franchisor–franchisee relationship is the formation of national and international associations by franchisors. This provides a forum for the exchange of information, ideas and experiences. Franchisors learn from each other's experiences and tend to adopt what, from their view, conforms to a notion of 'best practice'. Given that franchisees take on contracts formulated by the franchisor, this sophistication and monopolization by the franchisor could act increasingly to shift the balance of power in the relationship.

Allied to this is the increasing development of an industry of specialist business services capable of advising and acting for franchisors. The fields of law and finance are examples, where the primary clients for solicitors and banks are the franchisors. Against this, we may be witnessing the growing use of collective strength by franchisees. In the UK recently, the Franchise Advice and Consultancy Trade Association has been formed to act as a trade association for franchisees.

No doubt the delicate relationship between franchisor and franchisee will continue to evolve and adapt to changing circumstances. Only a few years ago, there was evidence to suggest that franchising might only feature in the early stage growth programmes of young companies who would later revert to more conventional patterns of managing their distribution. This no longer appears the case – franchising is here to stay but can only continue to prosper as long as franchisors have the foresight to leave sufficient freedom in franchise agreements to continue to motivate and reward franchisees.

Key points

- Franchises can and do fail.
- Changes in the future may erode franchisee independence.
- Franchising is likely to grow with the continuous expansion of service in the industries.

9

Useful resources in establishing your franchise

Outline

This chapter looks at:

- the British Franchise Association (BFA)
- the membership of the BFA
- franchise trade associations
- professional services

Introduction

As stated at the onset, the purpose of this book has been to guide you to the possibilities of owning your own franchise business, either as a franchisor or a franchisee. By presenting the various aspects and issues involved in this method of business, you now have the knowledge to make a firm decision on whether or not to continue with the possibility of franchising.

This chapter will present to you the resources available to convert your general ideas and convictions into a manageable and successful reality. From financial matters to general management, each aspect of your business plan can be developed by professionals trained not only in their particular field, but also in the area of franchising, to ensure the feasibility and achievement of your business endeavours.

The directory to follow is a comprehensive listing of agencies and professional services available to assist you, the appropriate contact, and the specific services offered. So although this chapter signifies the end of this guide, it does signify the true beginning of your business!

Franchise associations in the United Kingdom

The British Franchise Association

In 1977, the BFA was formed to fulfil two critical tasks: the first, to promote franchising, within the UK, as a viable business opportunity; the second, to establish strict ethical standards to guide and protect those either directly involved or serving in the franchise sector.

Stemming from these initial purposes, the BFA has become the main representing body of franchisors. It has become the authority in responsible franchising, the dispatcher of information and expertise, and the initiator in developing critical policies in franchising.

The BFA can offer the individual franchisor/franchisee general assistance and specific advice throughout each phase of establishing the business, through its educational programmes and seminars, regular meetings and newsletters, exhibitions, and its large and varied membership.

Following is the code of ethics which governs the activities of its members, and a list of the members which comprise the BFA.

For further information on the BFA and the services it can offer your specific interests, contact:

The British Franchise Association
Thames View
Newton Road
Henley-on-Thames
Oxon RG9 1HG
Tel: 0491 578049/578050
Fax: 0491 573517

The Franchise Consultants Association

The FCA was established in 1986 to establish and develop high ethical standards in the field of franchise consultancy and to identify those who are properly qualified to register as franchise consultants. Members of the FCA must have a proven record of experience in franchising and a reputation of meeting all standards in their business operations.

In general, the consultant can assist the potential franchisor in determining the best method of developing and establishing the business. Specifically, the consultant can conduct feasibility studies, preparation of the business plan, assessment of the necessary financial requirements, and recruitment and training. Through working with a member of the FCA, you are guaranteed the highest degree of expertise and confidentiality.

General guidance and specific information can be obtained by contacting:

Franchise Consultants Association
James House
37 Nottingham Road
London SW17 7EA
Tel: 081 767 1371
Fax: 081 767 2211

British Franchise Association

Code of ethics

1 The BFA's Code of Advertising Practice shall be based on that established by the Advertising Standards Association and shall be modified from time to time in accordance with alterations notified by the ASA.

   The BFA will subscribe fully to the ASA Code unless, on some specific issue, it is resolved by a full meeting of the Council of the BFA that the ASA is acting against the best interests of the public and of franchising business in general on that specific issue, in this case the BFA will be required to formally notify the ASA, setting out the grounds for disagreement.

2 No member shall sell, offer for sale, or distribute any product or render any service, or promote the sale or distribution thereof, under any representation or condition (including the use of the name of a 'celebrity') which has the tendency, capacity, or effect of misleading or deceiving purchasers or prospective purchasers.

3 No member shall imitate the trademark, trade name, corporate identity, slogan, or other mark or identification of another

franchisor in any manner or form that would have the tendency or capacity to mislead or deceive.

4 Full and accurate written disclosure of all information material to the franchise relationship shall be given to prospective franchisees within a reasonable time prior to the execution of any binding document.

5 The franchise agreement shall set forth clearly the respective obligations and responsibilities of the parties and all other terms of the relationship, and be free from ambiguity.

6 The franchise agreement and all matters basic and material to the arrangement and relationship thereby created, shall be in writing and executed copies thereof given to the franchisee.

7 A franchisor shall select and accept only those franchisees who, upon reasonable investigation, possess the basic skills, education, personal qualities, and adequate capital to succeed. There shall be no discrimination based on race, colour, religion, national origin or sex.

8 A franchisor shall exercise reasonable surveillance over the activities of his franchisees to the end that the contractual obligations of both parties are observed and the public interest safeguarded.

9 Fairness shall characterize all dealings between a franchisor and its franchisees. A franchisor shall give notice to its franchisee of any contractual breach and grant reasonable time to remedy default.

10 A franchisor shall make every effort to resolve complaints, grievances and disputes with its franchisees with good faith and good will through fair and reasonable direct communication and negotiation.

Criteria for membership with the British Franchise Association

Full membership

Franchisors are required to submit a completed application form, including disclosure document, franchise agreement, prospectus, accounts, etc., and provide proof of a correctly constituted pilot scheme successfully operated for at least one year, financed and managed by the applicant company. In addition, evidence of successful franchising over a subsequent two-year period with at least four franchisees is required.

Register of associates

As for Full Membership, including disclosure document, franchise agreement, prospectus, accounts, pilot scheme, etc., but with evidence of successful franchising for a period of one year with at least one franchisee.

In addition substantial companies with more than 25 company-owned outlets offering a franchise concept which is a replica of the existing business, with a separate franchise division, correctly constructed agreement, pilot scheme, prospectus and accounts but without a franchisee on station at the time of application, will also be eligible under this category.

Overseas members

Franchisors with an established franchise outside the UK are required to submit a completed application form including disclosure document, franchise agreement, prospectus, accounts, etc., and state the method of franchising in the UK (e.g. master licence, joint venture, subsidiary). In addition companies must supply evidence of a UK market survey and be Full Members of their National Association.

Early development category

This is a listing of companies at a very early stage of developing a franchise operation.

Affiliate listing

This is a list of professional and other advisers who are experienced in the franchising concept and have carried out satisfactory contracts with at least two existing BFA Full Members.

Members

Accounting Centre (The)
(A. Paris)
Elscot House
Arcadia Avenue
London N3 2JE
Tel: 081 349 3191

Alan Paul Hairdressing plc
(M. Rowland)
164 New Chester Road
Birkenhead
Merseyside L41 9BG
Tel: 051 666 1060

Alfred Marks (Franchise) Ltd
(Mrs L. Penniston)
Adia House
84–86 Regent Street
London W1A 1AL
Tel: 071 437 7855

Alpine Soft Drinks plc
(J. Flanagan)
Richmond Way
Chelmsley Wood
Birmingham B37 7TT
Tel: 021 7706816

Apollo Window Blinds Ltd
(J. Watson)
80 Johnstone Avenue
Cardonald Industrial Estate
Glasgow G52 4YH
Tel: 041 810 3021

Autela Components Ltd
(R. Taylor)
Regal House
Birmingham Road
Stratford upon Avon
Warks CV37 0BN
Tel: 0789 414545

Avis Rent A Car Ltd
(M. McInerney)
Trident House
Station Road
Hayes
Middlesex UB3 4DJ
Tel: 081 848 8765

Balmforth & Partners
(Franchises) Ltd
(S. Watson)
10 Bank Street
Norwich NR2 4SE
Tel: 0603 666506

Bath Doctor (The)
(M. H. Robertson)
Suite 5
Britannia House
Leagrove Road
Luton
Beds LU3 1RJ
Tel: 0582 459 336

Body & Face Place
(H. Miller)
164 New Chester Road
Birkenhead
Merseyside L41 9BG
Tel: 051 666 1060

Brewer & Turnbull Removals
(D. Boon)
Holme Road
Bamber Bridge
Preston
Lancs PR5 6BP
0772 626555

Britannia Business Sales Ltd
(J. G. Thompson)
Britannia Buildings
Park Gate
Bradford
W Yorkshire BD1 5BS
Tel: 0274 722977

British Damp Proofing
(A. Haslam)
The Old School
Fleetwood Road
Esprick
Preston PR4 3HJ
Tel: 039 136 441

Budget Rent-A-Car
International Inc
(N. Summerville)
41 Marlowes
Hemel Hempstead
Herts HP1 1LD
Tel: 0442 232555

Burgerking (UK) Ltd
(Mrs F. Rose)
20 Kew Road
Richmond
Surrey TW9 2NA
Tel: 081 940 6046

Chemical Express
(R. Jackson)
Ninian Way
Tame Valley Ind Est
Tamworth
Staffs B77 5DZ
Tel: 0827 251431

Circle 'C' Stores Ltd
(J. Wormull)
24 Fitzalan Road
Roffey
Horsham
W Sussex RH13 6AA
Tel: 0403 210450

Circle 'K' (UK) Ltd
(D. Ellis-Jones)
Fareham Point
Wickham Road
Fareham
Hants PO16 7BU
Tel: 0329 822666

City Link Transport Holdings
Ltd
(R. Thomas)
Batavia Road
Sunbury on Thames
Middlesex TW16 5LR
Tel: 0932 788799

Clarks Shoes Ltd
(P. Monaghan)
40 High Street
Street
Somerset BA16 0YA
Tel: 0458 43131

Coca Cola Export Corporation
(The)
(J. C. Moynihan)
Please note: No further
franchises available.

Colour Counsellors Ltd
(Mrs V. Stourton)
3 Dovedale Studios
465 Battersea Park Road
London SW11 4LR
Tel: 071 978 5023

Command Performance Int Ltd
(J. G. Macaulay)
256 High Street
Slough
Berks SL1 1JU
Tel: 0753 822645

Computa Tune
(A. Whittaker)
9 Petre Road
Clayton Park
Clayton le Moors
Accrington
Lancs BB5 5JB
Tel: 0254 391792/385891

Computerland Europe SA
(Tim Barnsley)
Windsor Crown House
7 Windsor Road
Slough
Berks SL1 2DX
Tel: 0753 512123

Country Rose Management
(Franchise) Ltd
(N. J. Ramsden)
Country Properties
41a High Street
Baldock
Herts SG7 5NP
Tel: 0462 896148

Crown Eyeglass plc
(J. Lee)
Glenfield Park
Northrop Avenue
Blackburn
Lancs BB1 5QF
Tel: 0254 51535

Dampcure/Woodcure 30
(B. Roberts)
Darley House
Cow Lane
Garston
Watford
Herts WD2 6PH
Tel: 0923 663322

Don Millers Hot Bread Kitchens
(G. Paterson)
166 Bute Street Mall
Arndale Centre
Luton
Beds LU1 2TL
Tel: 0582 422781

Dyno-Services Ltd
(N. Drage)
Zockoll House
143 Maple Road
Surbiton
Surrey KT6 4BJ
Tel: 081 549 9711

Euroclean
(J. Hopkinson)
13 The Office Village
4 Romford Road
London E15 4BZ
Tel: 081 519 3045

Everett Masson & Furby Ltd
(Mrs J. Brooker)
18 Walsworth Road
Hitchin
Herts SG4 9SP
Tel: 0462 32377

Fastframe Franchises Ltd
(Mrs M. Hewison)
International Centre
Netherton Park
Stannington
Northd NE6 6EF
Tel: 067089 797

Fersina International Ltd
(P. S. Hinchcliffe)
Fersina House
Industry Road
Carlton Industrial Estate
Carlton
Barnsley
S Yorks S70 3NH
Tel: 0226 728310

Francesco Group
(F. Dellicompagni)
Woodings Yard
Bailey Street
Stafford ST17 4BG
Tel: 0785 47175

GBC Buildings for Leisure
(C. Edwards)
Lye Head
Bewdley
Worcs DY12 2UX
Tel: 0299 266361/266337

Global Building Maintenance
Management Services
(K. Wearn)
8–10 High Street
Sutton
Surrey SM1 1HN
Tel: 081 642 0054

Gun-Point Ltd
(G. Jones)
Thavies Inn House
3/4 Holborn Circus
London EC1N 2PL
Tel: 071 353 6167

Holiday Inns International
(Mrs L. Bowyer)
Woluwe Office Park 1
Rue Neerveld 101
PO Box 2
1200 Brussels
Belgium
Tel: 02 773 5511

Hometune Ltd
(R. Deslandes)
77 Mount Ephraim
Tunbridge Wells
Kent TN4 8BS
Tel: 0892 510532

Interlink Express Parcels Ltd
(A. P. Gent)
Brunswick Court
Brunswick Square
Bristol BS2 8PE
Tel: 0272 426900

In-Toto Ltd
(M. Eccleston)
Wakefield Road
Gilderstone
Leeds LS27 0QW
Tel: 0532 524131

Kall-Kwik Printing (UK) Ltd
(A. Quail)
Kall-Kwik House
106 Pembroke Road
Ruislip
Middlesex HA4 8NW
Tel: 08956 32700

Keith Hall Hairdressing
(R. B. Gosnell)
199–121 Derby Road
Long Eaton
Nottingham NG10 4LA
Tel: 0602 729914

Kentucky Fried Chicken
(W. Girling)
88/97 High Street
Brentford
Middlesex TW8 8BG
Tel: 081 569 7070

Knobs & Knockers Franchising
Ltd
(J. R. Staddon)
Hathaway House
7d Woodfield Road
London W9 2EA
Tel: 071 289 4764

Kwik Strip (UK) Ltd
(I. Chivers)
PO Box 1087
Summerleaze
Church Road
Winscombe
Avon BS25 1BH
Tel: 093484 3100

The Late Late Supershop (UK)
Ltd
(D. Shannon)
132–152 Powis Street
Woolwich
London SE18 6NL
Tel: 081 854 2000

Master Thatchers Ltd
(R. C. West)
Rose Tree Farm
29 Nine Mile Ride
Finchampstead
Wokingham
Berks RG11 4QD
Tel: 0734 734203

111

Metro-Rod plc
(J. L. B. Harris)
Metro House
Churchill Way
Macclesfield
Cheshire SK11 6AY
Tel: 0625 34444

Mixamate Holdings Ltd
(P. Bates)
54 Beddington Lane
Croydon
Surrey CR9 4QD
Tel: 081 689 5500

Mobiletuning Ltd
(A. R. Rowntree)
The Gate House
Lympne Ind Park
Lympne
Hythe
Kent CT21 4LR
Tel: 0303 62419

Molly Maid UK
(M. Tall)
Hamilton Road
Slough
Berks SL1 4QY
Tel: 0753 23388/35343

Motabiz (Franchising) Ltd
(K. G. Oliver)
27–37 Craven Street
Northampton NN1 3EZ
Tel: 0604 231 777

Nationwide Investigations
(S. Withers)
86 Southwark Bridge Road
London SE1 0EX
Tel: 071 928 1799

Nectar Cosmetics Ltd
(B. Waring)
Carrickfergus Ind Est
Belfast Road
Carrickfergus
Co Antrim BT38 8PH
Tel: 09603 69133

Northern Dairies Ltd
(C. Wrigley)
Balne Lane
Wakefield WF2 0DL
Tel: 0924 290808

Olivers (UK) Ltd
(N. H. Allen)
Eagle Court
Harpur Street
Bedford MK40 1JZ
Tel: 0234 328181

Original Art Shop (The)
(M. Francis)
12 Southchurch Road
Southend-on-Sea
Essex SS1 2NE
Tel: 0702 460391

PDC Copyprint
(M. Marks)
1 Church Lane
East Grinstead
W Sussex RH19 3AZ
Tel: 0342 315321

Pass & Co
(Allen Winter)
Passco House
635 High Road
Leytonstone
London E11 4RD
Tel: 081 539 1105

Perfect Pizza
(R. Mendoza)
Pizza Restaurants
65 Staines Road
Hounslow
Middlesex TW3 3HW
Tel: 081 570 2323

Pip (UK) Ltd
(Mrs Lesley Sando)
Black Arrow House
2 Chandos Road
London NW10 6NF
Tel: 081 965 0700

Pizza Express Ltd
(J. Dell)
29 Wardour Street
London W1V 3HB
Tel: 071 437 7215

Poppies (UK) Ltd
(Mrs S. Rorstad)
31 Houndgate
Darlington
Co Durham DL1 5RH
Tel: 0325 488699

Practical Used Car Rental Ltd
(B. Agnew)
137/145 High Street
Bordesley
Birmingham B12 0JU
Tel: 021 772 8599

Prontaprint plc
(D. S. Mottershead)
Coniscliffe House
Coniscliffe Road
Darlington DL3 7EX
Tel: 0325 483333

Safeclean International
(D. H. Cook Ltd)
(D. Cook)
Delmae House
Home Farm
Ardington
Wantage
Oxon OX12 8PN
Tel: 0235 833022

Saks Hair (Holdings) Ltd
(D. Cheesebrough)
57 Coniscliffe Road
Darlington
Co Durham DL3 7EH
Tel: 0325 380333

Servicemaster Ltd
(M. Phillipson)
308 Melton Road
Leicester LE4 7SL
Tel: 0533 610761

Singer SDL Ltd
(M. I. Copping)
91 Colman Road
Leicester LE5 4LE
Tel: 0533 769471

Sketchley Recognition Express
Ltd
(Sketchley Business Services
Group)
(T. A. Howorth)
PO Box 7
Rugby Road
Hinckley
Leics LE10 2NE
Tel: 0455 38133

Snap-On-Tools Ltd
(M. Lancaster)
Palmer House
150–154 Cross Street
Sale
Cheshire M33 1AQ
Tel: 061 969 0126

Snappy Snaps (UK) Ltd
(T. MacAndrews)
11/12 Glenthorne Mews
Glenthorne Road
Hammersmith
London W6 0LJ
Tel: 081 741 7474

Spud-U-Like Ltd
(T. Schlesinger/M. Porripp)
34/38 Standard Road
London NW10 6EU
Tel: 081 965 0182

Strachan Studio
(G. Strachan)
Cross Green Way
Cross Green Ind Estate
Leeds LS9 0RS
Tel: 0532 495694

Swinton Insurance
(Peter Lowe)
6 Great Marlborough Street
Manchester M1 5SW
Tel: 061 236 1222

Thorntons
(J. W. Thornton Ltd)
(R. E. Smith)
Derwent Street
Belper
Derbys DE5 1WP
Tel: 077 382 4181

Tie Rack Ltd
(A. Potter)
Capital Interchange Way
Brentford
Middlesex TW8 0EX
Tel: 081 995 1344

TNT (UK) Ltd Parcel Office
(K. Young)
TNT House
Abeles Way
Atherstone
Warks CV9 2RY
Tel: 0827 303030

Travail Employment Group Ltd
(C. Rogers)
42a Cricklade Street
Cirencester
Glos GL7 1JH
Tel: 0285 659201

Trust Parts
(R. F. Wilson)
Unit 7 Groundwell Ind Est
Crompton Road
Swindon
Wilts SN2 5AY
Tel: 0793 723749

Unigate Dairies Ltd
(D. Haynes)
14/40 Victoria Road
Aldershot
Hants GU1 11TH
Tel: 0252 24522

Uticolor (Great Britain) Ltd
(R. Dowdall)
Acton Business Centre
School Road
London NW10
Tel: 081 965 6869

Weigh & Save
(Miss F. Fulton)
3rd Floor
Bridgewater House
Whitworth Street
Manchester M1 6LU
Tel: 061 236 7374

Wetherby Training Services
(D. G. Button)
Flockton House
Audby Lane
Wetherby
W Yorks LS22 4FD
Tel: 0937 63940

Wimpy International Ltd
10 Windmill Road
Chiswick
London W4 1SD
Tel: 081 994 6454

Yves Rocher (London) Ltd
(B. Saunders)
664 Victoria Road
South Ruislip
Middlesex HA4 0NY
Tel: 081 845 1222

Register of associates

A1 Damproofing
(J. B. Pickup)
New Side Mill
Charnley Fold Lane
Bamber Bridge
Preston
Lancs PR5 6AA
Tel: 0772 35228

Alpine Double Glazing Ltd
(B. Duckett)
Alpine House
Honeypot Lane
Kingsbury
London NW9 9RU
Tel: 081 204 3393

Amtrak Express Parcels Ltd
(R. Baines)
Company House
Tower Hill
Bristol BS2 0EQ
Tel: 0272 272002

Autosheen Car Valeting Services
(UK) Ltd
(M. Shirran)
Unit 4
Everitt Close
Denington Industrial Estate
Wellingborough
Northants NN8 2QE
Tel: 0933 72347

Banson Tool Hire
(J. P. Sharp)
Pellon Lane
Halifax HX1 5SB
Tel: 0422 331177

Berni Restaurants
(P. Whittle)
Oxford House
97 Oxford Road
Uxbridge UB8 1HX
Tel: 0895 70955

Blinkers
(M. P. Gower)
Consort Court
Off High Street
Fareham
Hants PO16 7AL
Tel: 0329 230580

Cico Chimney Linings Ltd
(R. J. Hadfield)
Westleton
Saxmundham
Suffolk IP17 3BS
Tel: 0728 73608

Clothesline
(Ms M. McGinn)
248 Seaward Street
Glasgow G41 1NG
Tel: 041 429 1433

Coffeeman Management Ltd
(S. Bayless)
73 Woolsbridge Ind Park
Wimborne
Dorset BH21 6SU
Tel: 0202 823501

Coppernob
(Ms C. Cameron)
95 Great Portland Street
London W1N 5RA
Tel: 071 436 3600

Countrywide Garden
  Maintenance Services
(M. Stott)
154–200 Stockport Road
Cheadle
Ches SK8 2DP
Tel: 061 428 4444

Dash Ltd
(F. Cox)
PO Box 5
Rowdell Road
Northolt
Middlesex UB5 5QT
Tel: 081 845 7777

Direct Salon Services Ltd
(W. Witcombe)
Newport Way
Cannon Park
Middlesbrough
Cleveland TS1 5JW
Tel: 0642 217978

Driver Hire
(J. P. Bussey)
West End House
Legrams Lane
Bradford BD7 7NH
Tel: 0274 726002

Duty Driver
(T. M. Bedford)
42A Station Road
Twyford
Berks RG10 9NT
Tel: 0734 320200

European Personal Associates
(N. Schollick)
Owl's Barn
Dorney Wood Road
Burnham
Bucks SL1 8EH
Tel: 0628 604814

Fires & Things Ltd
(B. Simpson)
Heat House
4 Brighton Road
Horsham
W Sussex RH13 5BA
Tel: 0403 56227

House of Colour
(Miss S. P. M. Fox-Ness)
4 Dudrich House
Princes Lane
London N10 3LU
Tel: 081 444 3621

Kansas Fried Chicken
(H. Yehia)
130A Wilmslow Road
Handforth
Cheshire SK9 3LQ
Tel: 0625 531 517

Leadstyle
(D. F. Underwood)
Roundwood
Sparken Hill
Worksop
Notts S80 1AP
Tel: 0909 475599

M & B Marquees
(J. Mansfield)
Unit 16
Swinborne Court
Burnt Mills Industrial Est
Basildon
Essex SS13 1QA
Tel: 0268 728361

Mainly Marines Franchising Ltd
(J. Driscoll)
6 Trojan Way
Croydon
Surrey CR0 4XL
Tel: 081 681 8421

Merryweathers
(L. Bird)
109 Hersham Road
Walton on Thames
Surrey KT12 1RN
Tel: 0932 247368

Professional Appearance
  Services Ltd
(D. Cook)
Unit 3
Avon Reach
Monkton Hill
Chippenham SN15 1EE
Tel: 02549 444182

PVC Vendo
(I. J. Calhoun)
215 East Lane
Wembley
Middlesex HA0 3NG
Tel: 081 908 1234

Quill Group
(Mrs J. Needham)
Harbro House
Okell Street
Runcorn WA7 5AP
Tel: 0928 580007

Re-Nu Ltd
(M. Weeraratne)
130 Stoneleigh Avenue
Worcester Park
Surrey KT4 8XZ
Tel: 081 330 6148

Stained Glass Overlay
(Steve Lawrence)
PO Box 65
Norwich NR6 6EJ
Tel: 0603 485454

Team Audio Ltd
(The Diamond Stylus Company Ltd)
(G. A. Edmondson)
Mochdre Industrial Estate
Colwyn Bay
Clwyd LL28 5HD
Tel: 0492 49272

Ventrolla Ltd
(R. W. Tunnicliffe)
51 Tower Street
Harrogate
N Yorks HG1 1HS
Tel: 0423 567004

Tune Up
(B. Skan)
23 High Street
Bagshot
Surrey GU19 5AF
Tel: 0276 51199

Franchise trade associations around the world

Australia

Franchisors Association of
Australia
6a Post Office Street
Pymble 2073, NSW
Australia
Tel: 02 449 5311

Canada

Association of Canadian
Franchisors
595 Bay Street
1050 Toronto, Ontario
Canada M5G 2C2
Tel: 416 595 5005

Belgium

Association Belge du Franchising
60 rue St Bernard
b. 1606 Bruxelles
Belgium
Tel: 322 537 30 60

Denmark

Dansk Franchisegiver-Forening
Sjaelsmarkvej 1B
DK 2970 Hoersholm
Denmark
Tel: 45 02765064

119

Eire

Irish Franchise Association
13 Frankfield Terrace
Summerhill South
Cork, Eire
Tel: 021 270859/50

EEC

European Franchise Federation
5 Avenue de Broqueville
b. 1150 Bruxelles
Belgium
Tel: 322 736 64 64

France

Federation Française de la
Franchise
9 Bd des Italiens
75002 Paris
France
Tel: 1 42 60 00 22

Holland

Nederlandse Franchise
Vereniging
Arubalaan 4, 1213 Vg Hilversum
Holland
Tel: 35 83 39 34

Italy

Associazione Italiana del
Franchising
Carso di Porta Nuova, 3
Milano 20121
Italy
Tel: 392 650 779

Japan

Japan Franchise Association
Elsa Building, 3-13-12
Roppongi, Minato-Ku
Tokyo, Japan
Tel: 408 17 76

Norway

Norwegian Franchise Association
Astveitskogen 41
Tertnes Bergen 5084
Norway

South Africa

South African Franchise
Association
PO Box 18498
Hillbrow 2038
South Africa
Tel: 011 642 2921

Sweden

Swedish Franchise Association
PO Box 26002
S–100 41 Stockholm
Sweden
Tel: 08 723 05 33

Switzerland

Swiss Franchise Association
Avenue du Mail 5
CH–1205 Geneve
Switzerland
Tel: 022 28 36 38

United States of America

International Franchise
Association
Suite 900, 1350 New York
Avenue, NW
Washington DC 20005
Tel: 202 628 8000
Fax: 202 628 0812

West Germany

Deutscher Franchise-Verband
St Paul Strasse 9
8000 Munchen 2
West Germany
Tel: 0 89 53 50 27

UK Representative
Martin Mendelsohn
Adlers
22–26 Paul Street
London EC2A 4JH
Tel: 071 481 9100
Fax: 071 247 4701

Professional services

Following is a list of professional agencies which can assist you in specific areas of franchising. All firms listed are affiliates of the BFA.

Bankers

Bank of Scotland plc
(P. Smith)
38 Threadneedle Street
London SW1Y 4QY
Tel: 071 601 6504

Barclays Bank plc
(J. S. Perkins)
Corporate Marketing Dept
Ground Floor
168 Fenchurch Street
London EC3P 3HD
Tel: 071 283 8989

Clydesdale Bank plc
(G. G. Strachan)
PO Box 43
30 St Vincent Place
Glasgow G1 2HL
Tel: 041 248 7070

Lloyds Bank plc
(Chris Walker)
Franchise Unit
Small Business Services
Mezzanine Floor
71 Lombard Street
London EC3P 3BS
Tel: 071 626 1500

Midland Bank plc
(Dai Rees)
Small & Medium Enterprise Unit
Marketing Department
PO Box 2
41 Silver Street Head
Sheffield S1 3GG
Tel: 0742 529037

National Westminster Bank plc
Retail Banking Services
Franchise Section
2nd Floor
75 Cornhill
London WC3V 3NN
Tel: (Peter Stern 071 280 4262)
     (Ray Leach 071 280 4263)
     (John Sheppard
     071 280 4596)
     (Tony Ellingham
     071 280 4264)

The Royal Bank of Scotland plc
(T. C. Bowyer)
PO Box 348
42 Islington High Street
London N1 8XL
Tel: 071 833 2121

The Royal Bank of Scotland plc
(R. Campbell)
42 St Andrew Square
Edinburgh EH2 2YE
Tel: 031 556 8555

The Royal Bank of Scotland plc
(M. Whittington)
Centurion House
129 Deansgate
Manchester
M3 3WR
Tel: 061 236 8585

Chartered accountants

BDO Binder Hamlyn
(C. R. J. Foley)
Ballantine House
168 West George Street
Glasgow G2 2PT
Tel: 041 248 3761

Brodie Brunton & Co
(R. Brunton)
185 Byres Road
Glasgow G12 8TS
Tel: 041 334 6162

Ernst & Young
(Brian A. Smith)
Rolls House
7 Rolls Buildings
Fetter Lane
London EC4A 1NH
Tel: 071 928 2000

KPMG Peat Marwick McLintock
(G. Hopkinson)
Aquis Court
31 Fishpool Street
St Albans
Herts AL3 4RF
Tel: 0727 43000

Kidsons
(D. V. Collins)
Carlton House
31–34 Railway Street
Chelmsford, Essex CM1 1NJ
Tel: 0245 269595

Neville Russell
(John Chastney)
246 Bishopsgate
London EC2M 4PB
Tel: 0603 617009

Price Waterhouse
(W. Clark)
Southwark Towers
32 London Bridge Street
London SE1 9SY
Tel: 071 407 8989

Touche Ross
(M. A. B. Jenks)
Hill House
1 Little New Street
London EC4A 3TR
Tel: 071 353 8011

Chartered surveyors

David Menzies-Taylor Placks
(M. Placks)
Leonard House
12 St George Street
Hanover Square
London W1R 9DF
Tel: 071 491 7777

Stewart Newiss
(J. F. Smith)
77 St Vincent Street
Glasgow G2 5TF
Tel: 041 226 4061

Development Agencies

Scottish Development Agency
(B. McVey)
120 Bothwell Street
Glasgow G2 7JP
Tel: 041 248 2700

Exhibition organizers

Blenheim Princedale Ltd
(Ms T. Jarvis)
Blenheim House
137 Blenheim Crescent
London W11 2EQ
Tel: 071 727 1929

123

Franchise consultants

Caltain Associates
(R. W. Crook)
Bridlepath House
Broken Gate Lane
Denham
Bucks UB9 4LB
Tel: 0895 834200

Ernst & Young
(Brian Smith)
Rolls House
7 Rolls Buildings
Fetter Lane
London EC4A 1NH
Tel: 071 928 2000

FMM Franchise & Licensing
Services Ltd
(Mike Matthews)
46/48 Thornhill Road
Streetly
Sutton Coldfield
West Midlands B74 3EH
Tel: 021 353 0031/2

Saffery Champness Consultancy
Services Ltd
(Dereck Ayling)
2 Chilbolton Avenue
Winchester
Hants SO22 5HH
Tel: 0962 69998

Stoy Hayward Franchising
(David Acheson)
8 Baker Street
London W1M 1DA
Tel: 071 486 5888

Media and communications

Business Franchise Magazine
(C. G. Bradbury)
Newspaper House
Tannery Lane
Penketh
Cheshire WA5 2UD
Tel: 092572 4234

Franchise World
(Robert Riding)
James House
37 Nottingham Road
London SW17 7EA
Tel: 081 767 1371

Murray Maltby Walker & West
(G. Peacock)
Belmont House
20 Wood Lane
Headingley
Leeds LS6 2AE
Tel: 0532 744447

Patent & trade mark agents

Ladas & Parry
(Iain C. Baillie)
52–54 High Holborn
London WC1V 6RR
Tel: 071 242 5566

Lawyers

Adlers
(Martin Mendelsohn/Manzoor
Ishani)
22–26 Paul Street
London EC2A 4JH
Tel: 071 481 9100

Bird Semple & Crawford Herron
(Malcolm J. Gillies)
249 West George Street
Glasgow G2 4RB
Tel: 041 221 7090

Bristows Cooke & Carpmael
(E. J. Nodder)
10 Lincolns Inn Fields
London WC2A 3BP
Tel: 071 242 0462

Brodies
(J. C. A. Voge)
15 Atholl Crescent
Edinburgh EH3 8HA
Tel: 031 228 3777

Field Fisher Waterhouse
(Mark Abell)
Lincoln House
296–302 High Holborn
London WC1V 7JL
Tel: 071 831 9161

Forsyte Kerman
(R. D. Thornton)
79 New Cavendish Street
London W1M 8AQ
Tel: 071 637 8566

Glaisyers
(S. Pigden)
7 Rowchester Court
Whittall Street
Birmingham B4 6DZ
Tel: 021 200 2010

Hopkins & Wood
(D. Bigmore)
2–3 Cursitor Street
London EC4A 1NE
Tel: 071 404 0475

Howard Jones & Company
(G. E. Howard Jones)
32 Market Street
Hoylake
Wirral
Merseyside
Tel: 051 632 3411

Levy & Macrae
(T. Caplan)
13 Bath Street
Glasgow G2 1HZ
Tel: 041 331 2311

MacRoberts
(Michael Bell)
152 Bath Street
Glasgow G2 4TB
Tel: 041 332 9988

Mundays
(Ray Walley)
Speer House
40 The Parade
Glaygate
Esher
Surrey KT10 0NY
Tel: 0372 67272

Needham & James
(John H. Pratt)
Windsor House
Temple Row
Birmingham B2 5LF
Tel: 021 200 1188

Owen White
(Anton Bates)
Johnson House
Browells Lane
Feltham
Middlesex TW13 7EQ
Tel: 081 890 0505

Peters & Peters
(Raymond Cannon)
2 Harewood Place
Hanover Square
London W1R 9HB
Tel: 071 629 7991

Stephenson Harwood
(J. Schwarz)
One St Paul's Churchyard
London EC4M 8SH
Tel: 071 329 4422

Key points

- The BFA can offer assistance to franchisees as well as franchisors.
- Franchising has good international links.
- Franchising is now surrounded by a host of professional services including banks, accountants, lawyers and consultants.

APPENDIX 1

Franchise agreement - short form

By John Adams and
K.V. Prichard Jones

REPRINTED FROM FRANCHISING: PRACTICE AND PRECEDENTS IN BUSINESS FORMAT FRANCHISING (SECOND EDITION) BY KIND PERMISSION OF THE PUBLISHERS, BUTTERWORTHS

Dated .... 19......

1 Parties

.... whose [registered office *or* principal place of business] is at (*address*) ('the Franchisor') (1)

.... whose [registered office *or* principal place of business] is at (*address*) ('the Franchisee') (2)

2 Definitions
The following terms shall have the following meanings:

2.1 'Advertising Contribution': ....% of Gross Turnover (as defined in clause [3.12] of the Conditions) of the Business

2.2 'Business': the use (for mutual benefit) of the Mark and the Know-How in the business of trading under the Permitted Name in the style and manner stipulated by the Franchisor for (*insert details of Business to be carried out*)

2.3 'Conditions': the Standard Conditions and Special Conditions (if any) annexed to this Agreement which shall be deemed to be incorporated in this Agreement in their entirety

2.4 'Continuing Fees': the franchise fees of ....% of Gross Turnover (as defined in clause [3.12] of the Conditions) of the Business

2.5 'Financial Year': each year during the Term ending on the .... (*year end date*)

2.6 'Initial Fee': the initial franchise fee of £........... (....... pounds)

2.7 'Know-How': the operational systems and methods of the Franchisor as divulged to the Franchisee from time to time during the Term

2.8 'Location': the premises shortly described as ...... or such other premises as are approved by the Franchisor during the Term

2.9 'Manual': the confidential written systems of and regulations for the operation of the Business issued and amended by the Franchisor from time to time during the Term incorporating part of the Know-How and deemed to form part of this Agreement (Serial Number ......)

2.10 'Mark': the [Legend] [and design] and the logos associated with the same and any additional or substitute Marks which the Franchisor shall deem suitable for the Business during the Term

2.11 'Minimum Package':

    2.11:1 The equipment products literature stock of all types and

    2.11:2 The minimum staff levels [at the location] stipulated in the manual from time to time during the Term

2.12 'Payment Dates':

    2.12:1 For the Initial Fee: on the signing of this Agreement

    2.12:2 For the Advertising Contributions and the Continuing Fees: the [tenth] day of each [calendar month] during the Term in respect of the Business during the immediately preceding calendar month

2.13 'Permitted Name': the permitted business name of the Franchisee which shall be '......'

2.14 'Term': ...... years from .... 19 ...... (the Commencement Date) and expiring on .... 19...... (the Expiry Date) unless sooner determined as provided in the Conditions

2.15 'Territory': the geographical area of (*insert description of area*) [and shown edged red on the map annexed to this Agreement]

3 The Right
In consideration of the payment of the Initial Fee the Insurance Premium the Advertising Contribution and the Continuing Fees by the Franchisee to the Franchisor and of and subject to the agreements on the part of the Franchisee in this Agreement the Franchisor grants to the Franchisee the right of using the Mark and the Know-How only:

3.1 In the Business

3.2 At and from the Location

3.3 Within the Territory

3.4 For the Term

3.5 Under the Permitted Name

3.6 In accordance with the Manual

Dated .... day of .... 19 ......

Signed by .... (*name of director*) for and on behalf of .... (*name of Franchisor*)

Signed by .... (*name of director*) for and on behalf of .... (*name of Franchisee*)

STANDARD CONDITIONS

1 Title
The Franchisor warrants that it is the beneficial owner of the Mark and Know-How

2 Franchisor's obligations
The Franchisor agrees as follows:

2.1 Training
To provide within 90 days of this date at a place chosen by the Franchisor training in the conduct of the Business for one director of the Franchisee and all the initial employees of the Franchisee the cost of which is included in the Initial Fee

2.2 Manual

To issue the Franchisee with the Manual and to update it (provided the same shall remain the property of the Franchisor)

2.3 Advertising

To undertake an advertising and promotional programme for the Mark in selected areas of the British Isles in such manner as it considers appropriate using the Advertising Contribution

2.4 Advertising bank account

To pay the Advertising Contribution (together with similar contributions from [stores *or* outlets] owned by the Franchisor) into a separate bank account of the Franchisor maintained for that purpose only

2.5 Expenses

To issue to the Franchisee an account of the total expenditure by the Franchisor on advertising and promotion in each Financial Year of the Term provided that the Franchisor shall be entitled to recoup at any time from the total of the Advertising Contribution from all its franchisees in any year any excess of such expenditure over the total of receipts of the Advertising Contributions in previous or future years

2.6 Exclusive

Not to undertake on its own behalf nor to grant any franchise to any other person or entity in respect of the Business in the Territory (subject as appears later in these Conditions)

2.7 Information

Throughout the Term to consider and respond to all reasonable requests from the Franchisee for information and assistance concerning the Business

2.8 Supply Conditions

To procure that products for the Business shall be supplied to the Franchisee by the Franchisor or its approved suppliers on the same terms as those supplies to [stores *or* outlets] operated by the Franchisor itself in the United Kingdom

[2.9 Additional sales

To permit the Franchisee to sell such equipment and similar items in addition to the Minimum Package in order to satisfy specific orders or demand subject to the prior approval by the Franchisor of such equipment and other items]

3 Franchisee's obligations

The Franchisee agrees throughout the Term:

3.1 Training first

3.1:1   Not to commence the Business until [one director of] the Franchisee and all its senior employees have received training from and have been approved as competent by the Franchisor

3.1:2   To notify the Franchisor whenever it employs new staff in the Business

3.1:3   Not to permit any person to be employed in the Business unless such person is first trained and approved as competent by the Franchisor

3.1:4   To procure that all its executives and employees attend further training during the Term when required by the Franchisor

3.2 Registered user

Where necessary to become the registered user of the Mark or to execute on demand from the Franchisor such formal licence for records purposes as may be required in the United Kingdom

3.3 Authority

To display at the Location and on all stationery and any literature used by the Franchisee the text stipulated in the Manual from time to time disclosing that the Franchisee is licensed by the Franchisor and is not a branch or agent of the Franchisor

3.4 Mark

3.4:1   Constantly to protect and promote the goodwill attached to the Mark (which the Franchisee acknowledges is of great value)

3.4:2   To hold any additional goodwill generated by the Franchisee for the Mark or the Permitted Name as bare trustee for the Franchisor

3.4:3   Not to cause or permit any damage to the Mark or the title of the Franchisor to it or assist others to do so

3.4:4   Not to use the Mark the Know-How or the Permitted Name except directly in the Business

3.4:5   Not to use the Mark the Know-How or the Permitted Name in any manner after the Term or other sooner determination of the Agreement

3.4:6   Not to use the Mark or any derivation of the same in the corporate name (if any) of the Franchisee

3.5 Secrecy

Not at any time during or after the Term:

3.5:1   to divulge to any third party any information concerning the Business the Franchisor the Know-How or any other systems or methods of the Franchisor used in the Business (especially that contained in the Manual)

3.5:2   to copy in any way in any part of the Manual

3.6 Disclosure

Not to employ any person in the Business until that person has signed a non-disclosure undertaking in the form approved by the Franchisor from time to time

3.7 Volume

To use its best endeavours to achieve the greatest volume of business for the Business at the Location consistent with good service to the public

3.8 No other business

Not without the prior approval of the Franchisor:

3.8:1   to permit any other business venture to operate or trade at or from the Location

3.8:2   to extend the scope or range of the Business at the Location

3.8:3   to engage directly or indirectly in any other business other than the Business

3.9 No illegal use

Not to engage in any activities in the Business which may be contrary to law or governments or other regulations

3.10 Payments

To pay the Initial Fee the Continuing Fees and the Advertising Contribution (without demand deduction or set-off) to the Franchisor (or as it directs) on each of the Payment Dates (time being of the essence)

3.11 VAT contingency

Whenever applicable to pay to the Franchisor VAT or any other tax or duty replacing the same during the Term charged or calculated on the amount of the Initial Fee the Continuing Fees and the Advertising Contribution

3.12 Calculations

To calculate the Continuing Fees and the Advertising Contribution on the gross turnover of the Business arising

128

directly or indirectly from the conduct of the Business in the Territory during each calendar week of the Term (and for any period less than a complete calendar week) and gross turnover shall include

3.12:1 all credit sales of whatever nature whether or not the Franchisee has received payment of the outstanding accounts by the Payment Date relevant to the week when such credit sales were made

3.12:2 all cash sales of whatever nature made but not invoiced by the Franchisee in each week

3.12:3 all services performed and business dealings whatsoever (other than purchases) made or conducted in the Territory by the Business during each week

But shall exclude

3.12:4 any VAT

3.12:5 any customer refunds or credits arising from the supply of defective goods or services or the like provided that such refunds or credits shall only be deducted from gross turnover in the calendar week in which they are paid or allowed to the customer

3.13 Service report

On each Monday of each week to post by first-class mail (or by electronic means if required by the Franchisor) to the Franchisor complete and accurate statements (in the form approved by the Franchisor in the Manual) of the sales made and services performed by the Business since the last such Payment Date

3.14 Accurate accounts

To keep accurate books and accounts in respect of the Business in accordance with good accountancy custom in the United Kingdom and the standards set out in the Manual and to:

3.14:1 Accountants
have them audited at the expense of the Franchisee once a year during the Term by the firm of Chartered Accountants nominated by the Franchisor

3.14:2 Audit
submit the whole of such audited accounts to the Franchisor within three months of the end of such year

3.14:3 Custody
keep them for not less than [3] years

3.14:4 Inspection
permit the Franchisor to inspect and take copies (at the expense of the Franchisor) of any financial information or records it requires (on reasonable prior notice in the event of inspection after normal business hours)

3.14:5 Financial Year
procure that each financial year or period of the Business shall be the same as the Financial Year

3.15 Discrepancies

In the event of discrepancies (amounting in total to more than [2%] per year of gross sales) in any such books or accounts to permit accountants nominated by the Franchisor but at the expense of the Franchisee to undertake audits of the same in each year of the Term of the Franchisor (at intervals at the discretion of the Franchisor) on reasonable notice and during normal business hours

3.16 VAT report

Within 14 days of submission or receipt to supply to the Franchisor a copy of each VAT return and/or assessment in respect of the Business

3.17 Conduct of the Business

Not to conduct the Business except:

3.17:1 Standards
In respect of services to the standards and quality and in the standard style and by the methods stipulated in the Manual from time to time

3.17:2 Regulations
In conformity with all relevant government or other regulations

3.17:3 Financial systems
Under proper and comprehensive financial systems and controls as approved or stipulated by the Franchisor

3.17:4 Venue
At or from the Location or such other venue first approved by the Franchisor

3.17:5 Inside Territory
Inside the Territory

[3.17:6 Equipment
With the equipment part of the Minimum Package in good and reliable condition]

[3.17:7 Staff
With the staff part of the minimum package at full complement and fully trained and approved by the Franchisor]

3.17:8 Dealerships
In accordance with the rules and regulations of any dealership or distributorship arrangements for any of the equipment or products dealt in by the Business

3.18 Insurance policy

3.18:1 To maintain and pay all premiums in respect of a comprehensive insurance policy (in terms approved by the Franchisor) issued by an insurer nominated by the Franchisor in respect of the Location for all items stored there and for the Business

3.18:2 To note on such policy that:

3.18:2.1 the Franchisor shall be covered by such policy in respect of all claims arising from activities at the Location or in the Business or of the Franchisee which are risks covered by such policy

3.18:2.2 the insurer shall notify the Franchisor in the event of any late premium payment by the Franchisee

3.19 Inspection of Premises

To permit the Franchisor or its representatives to inspect the Location at any time during the Term

3.20 Right notices

To affix such patent copyright or trade mark ownership notices to any stationery or literature used by the Franchisee in the Business as the Franchisor may require from time to time

3.21 Infringement indemnity

To indemnify the Franchisor from:

3.21:1 any alleged unauthorised use or infringement of any patent trade mark copyright or other intellectual property (other than the Mark and Know-How) by the Franchisee

3.21:2 any claim by any third party in respect of the conduct of the Business or the conduct or neglect of the Franchisee

3.21:3 any infringement by the Franchisee of any relevant regulations

3.22 Infringement notice

To notify the Franchisor of any suspected infringement of the intellectual property or other rights of the Franchisor and to take such reasonable action thereupon as the Franchisor directs at the expense of the Franchisor

3.23 Payment

Not to purchase any supplies [courses] products equipment or literature for the Business except from the Franchisor or (with the consent of the Franchisor) its approved suppliers to ensure even standards of quality of products and services from all the franchisees of the Franchisor and:

3.23:1 to pay the Franchisor for any equipment stationery or other items so purchased within 21 days of dispatch by the Franchisor

3.23:2 to pay promptly any other suppliers of the Franchisee in accordance with their usual terms and conditions

3.24 No sub-franchise

Not to grant any sub-franchise in respect of the Mark the Know-How or the Business

3.25 Promotions

3.25:1 To advertise the Business in the Territory in accordance with the requirements of the Franchisor set out in the Manual from time to time

3.25:2 (As part of such obligation) to expend not less than ......% of the gross turnover of the Business in each Financial Year upon local advertising and promotional activities

3.25:3 To participate in such promotional activities for the Business in the Territory as the Franchisor requires during the Term

3.26 Assignment

Not to assign transfer or otherwise deal with the Right or this Agreement or the Business in any way without the prior approval of the Franchisor which shall not be unreasonably withheld in the following circumstances:

3.26:1 if the proposed assignee is acceptable to the Franchisor and shall agree to be bound by the terms and conditions of the standard franchise agreement used by the Franchisor at the time of such proposed assignment for the residue of the Term and

3.26:2 if the Franchisee shall pay to the Franchisor the reasonable costs and expenses incurred by the Franchisor in the assessment of each proposed assignee

3.27 Director reliance

(As the Right has been granted to the Franchisee by the Franchisor in reliance upon the quality of the directors and shareholders of the Franchisee) not to permit any change in the same without the prior approval of the Franchisor which shall not be unreasonably withheld subject to the provisions in sub-clauses [3.26:1 and 3.26:2] of these conditions

3.28 Prices

3.28:1 Not to charge any customer any prices in excess of those stipulated in the Manual from time to time

3.28:2 Not to sell any items or provide any services to any person or entity associated with the Franchisee or its shareholders except at prices usually charged by the Franchisee to its non-connected customers

3.29 No competition

And for a period of [two] years afterwards:

3.29:1 Not to engage directly or indirectly in any capacity in any business venture competitive with or likely to damage the surviving goodwill of the Business in the Territory or in any territory any business venture competitive with any business of the other franchisee of the Franchisor

3.29:2 Not to solicit the customers or former customers of the Business with the intent of taking their custom

3.29:3 Not to employ any employee or former employees who were employed in the Business by the Franchisee or by the Franchisor or any other franchisee of the Franchisor

and to procure that all directors and shareholders of the Franchisee enter into direct covenants of similar content with the Franchisor

3.30 Grant back

To notify the Franchisor and provide full details of any improvements in the methods systems products or programmes described by the Franchisor in the Manual or employed in the Business and to permit the Franchisor to incorporate free of charge any such improvements in its Manual for the benefit of the Franchisor and all its franchisees.

[3.31 Premises

3.31:1 To maintain the Location in good decorative repair and condition

3.31:2 To alter the exterior and interior decoration signs and furnishings of the Location when required to do so by the Franchisor in accordance with any amendments it may make to the house style of the Business

3.31:3 To observe and perform all its obligations under any lease or tenancy of the Location]

4 Expiry procedure

On expiry or termination of this Agreement the Franchisee agrees:

4.1 Not to endeavour to surrender the telephones used in the Business nor to hinder the transfer of such telephones to such person as the Franchisor directs

4.2 To return to the Franchisor all stationery used in the Business

4.3 to return to the Franchisor all publicity promotional and advertising material

4.4 To return to the Franchisor the Manual in good condition and without having made any copy of the Manual

4.5 To sign such notification of cessation of use of the Mark as is necessary for recording at the Trade Marks Registry

4.6 To cease carrying on the Business immediately

4.7 (When the Franchisee is the tenant or lessee of the Franchisor at the Location) to surrender to the Franchisor the relevant tenancy agreement or lease immediately upon such expiry or termination and to vacate the Location immediately

5 Expiry financial procedure

The Franchisee agrees:

5.1 Four weeks prior to the expiry of the Term or three weeks after receipt of notice of termination of this Agreement to furnish to the Franchisor a complete and accurate up-to-date list of customers of the Business with estimates of turnover of the Business to such expiry or termination date and

5.2 Thereupon to pay the Continuing Fees and the Advertising Contribution on the estimated Gross Turnover to such date and

5.3 Not later than the first Friday after such date to pay to the Franchisor any additional amount of the Continuing Fees and the Advertising Contribution calculated on actual gross turnover of the Business to such date

6 Miscellaneous
It is further agreed between the parties:
6.1 Reservation of rights
6.1:1   All the rights not specifically and expressly granted to the Franchisee in this Agreement are reserved to the Franchisor

6.1:2   The Franchisor may grant a licence to any entity to manufacture any products in the Territory or elsewhere for use in connection with the Business or displaying the Mark or for other purposes (except in competition with the Franchisee in the Territory) without any liability to the Franchisee

6.2 Interest
Without prejudice to the rights of the Franchisor and the condition that the Initial Fee the Advertising Contribution and the Continuing Fees are paid on time (time being of the essence) all sums due to the Franchisor which are not paid on the due date shall bear interest from day to day at the annual rate of ......% over the current Bank plc daily base interest rate with a minimum of ......%

6.3 Payment not on time
In the event that the Franchisee fails to pay any money due to the Franchisor on time the Franchisor may
6.3:1   cease immediately to take orders from and to deliver goods and services to the Franchisee

6.3:2   afterwards impose whatever credit limit it considers appropriate in respect of the Business of the Franchisee

6.4 Receipt
The receipt of money by the Franchisor shall not prevent either of the parties questioning the correctness of any statement in respect of that money

6.5 Force majeure
Both parties shall be released from their respective obligations in the event of national emergency war prohibitive governmental regulations or if any other cause beyond the control of the parties shall render performance of the Agreement impossible provided that this clause shall only have effect at the discretion of the Franchisor except when such event renders performance impossible for a continuous period of [12] calendar months

6.6 Severance
In the event that any provision of this Agreement or these Conditions is declared by any judicial or other competent authority to be void voidable illegal or otherwise unenforceable [or indications of the same are received by either of the parties from any relevant competent authority] [the parties shall amend that provision in such reasonable manner as achieves the intention of the parties without illegality or the Franchisor may sever the offending provision from the same at its discretion *or* the remaining provisions of this Agreement shall remain in full force and effect unless the Franchisor in the Franchisor's discretion decides that the effect of such declaration is to defeat the original intention

of the parties in which event the Franchisor shall be entitled to terminate this Agreement by [30] days' notice to the Franchisee and the provisions of clause [4] shall apply accordingly]

6.7 Low sales
The Franchisor may terminate this Agreement in the event that reasonably substantial turnover (which shall be calculated by the Franchisor on the basis of demographic and socio-economic data in respect of the Territory and the performance of its other franchisees) arising from the Business at the Location is not achieved within two years of the Commencement Date of the Agreement or for a continuous period of twelve months at any time afterwards during the Term provided that the Franchisor shall have the right (but not the duty):
6.7:1   then to appoint management personnel to supervise the Business at the expense of the Business to assist the Franchisor to increase sales and/or

6.7:2   to reduce the area of the Territory in proportion to such sales

6.8 New outlets
6.8:1   In the event that the Franchisor decides that the Territory is sufficiently large geographically and has a sufficiently large population to justify one or more further outlets for the Business in the Territory it may notify the Franchisee of such decision and on receipt of such notice the Franchisee shall have the right to open such further outlet elsewhere than at the Location (in an area of the Territory nominated by the Franchisor) provided that the Franchisee informs the Franchisor within 90 days of such notice of its agreement to do so

6.8:2   In the event that the Franchisee fails to notify the Franchisor of such agreement within 90 days or fails to open such further outlet in the Territory within six months of such notice the Franchisor shall have the right to reduce the Territory to enable it to provide an exclusive area in which a new franchisee may trade using the Mark and the Know-How without liability to the Franchisee

6.9 Prior obligations
The expiration or termination of this Agreement shall not relieve either of the parties of their respective prior obligations or impair or prejudice their respective rights against the other.

6.10 Discretion
No decision exercise of discretion judgement opinion or approval of any matter mentioned in this Agreement or arising from it shall be deemed to have been made by the Franchisor except if in writing and shall be at its sole discretion unless otherwise expressly provided in this Agreement or these Conditions

6.11 Notice
6.11:1   Any notice to be served on either of the parties by the other shall be sent by prepaid recorded delivery or registered post (as the case may be) or by telex or by electronic mail and shall be deemed to have been received by the addressee within 72 hours of posting or 24 hours if sent by telex or by electronic mail to the correct telex or

electronic mail number of the addressee

6.11:2 Each of the parties shall notify the other of any change of address or number as soon as practicable and in any event within 48 hours of such change

6.12 No agency

The parties are not partners or joint venturers nor is the Franchisee able to act as the agent or to pledge the credit of the Franchisor in any way

6.13 Whole agreement

The Franchisee acknowledges that this Agreement and these Conditions contain the whole agreement between the parties and it had not relied upon any oral or written representations made to it by the Franchisor or its employees or agents and has made its own independent investigations into all matters relevant to the Business

6.14 Breach procedure

In the event that the Franchisee fails to observe or perform any of its obligations under this Agreement or these Conditions in any way then the Franchisor may terminate this Agreement on 30 days' written notice and

6.14:1 notwithstanding such notice period if the breach complained of is incapable of remedy this Agreement shall terminate absolutely on service of such notice

6.14:2 in every other case if the breach complained of is remedied to the satisfaction of the Franchisor within the notice period this Agreement shall not terminate

6.14:3 no waiver of any breach of those obligations shall constitute a waiver of any further or continuing breach of the same

6.15 Insolvency

If the Franchisee enters into liquidation or suffers a receiver to be appointed to it or to any of its assets or makes a composition with any of its creditors (or the equivalent in Scotland) the Franchisor may at any time afterwards terminate this Agreement on notice with immediate effect and:

6.15:1 no creditor agent representative or trustee of the Franchisee shall have the right to use the Mark or the Know-How or continue the Business without the prior consent of the Franchisor

6.15:2 until payment of all money due to the Franchisor from the Franchisee on any account the Franchisor shall have a lien on any of the stock literature or other products held by the Franchisee

6.16 Assignment

The Franchisor may assign charge or otherwise deal with this Agreement in any way

6.17 Renewal option

The Franchisee shall have the option to extend the Term for a further period of .... years commencing on the day following the Expiry Date subject to the following:

6.17:1 service of notice of extension by the Franchisee on the Franchisor not later than ...... calendar months prior to the Expiry Date and

6.17:2 payment by the Franchisee to the Franchisor not later than two calendar months prior to the Expiry Date of a renewal fee of ......% of gross turnover of the Business during 12 calendar months prior to the first day of the calendar month in which such notice is served or the then current Initial

Fee charged by the Franchisor to its franchisees (whichever is the less) and

6.17:3 proper performance and observance by the Franchisee of all its obligations under this Agreement throughout the Term and

6.17:4 execution by the Franchisee of a new franchise agreement in the standard form used by the Franchisor at the time of service of such notice in respect of the further period of ...... years without any option to renew

6.18 Further extension

In the event that any regulation requires the Franchisor to extend the Term beyond the period of a further ...... years as mentioned in clause [6.17] of these Conditions then the same provisions and procedure as set out there shall apply to any such subsequent extension.

6.19 Death or incapacity

6.19:1 In the event of the death of an individual Franchisee the personal representatives of the Franchisee shall have six calendar months from the date of death to notify the franchisor of their decision

6.19:1.1 to continue the Business whereupon such personal representatives shall be deemed to be proposed assignees of the Business or

6.19:1.2 to assign the Business to any of the heirs of the Franchisee or to a third party

whereupon the provisions set out in sub-clauses [3.26:1 and 3.26:2] of these Conditions shall apply

6.19:2 In the event of the incapacity of [the Franchisee or ...... (*the key director of the Franchise*)] at any time or after such death (but prior to any such decision by such personal representatives) the Franchisor shall have the right (but not the duty) to appoint management personnel to supervise the conduct of the Business (at the expense of the Business) to ensure that the Business shall operate in a satisfactory manner to preserve the goodwill of the Mark pending the recovery of the Franchisee or such decision

6.19:3 If so requested by the Franchisee (or the personal representatives of the Franchisee) the Franchisor may act as a non-exclusive agent for the sale of the Business and in such event shall be paid its expenses and fees as follows:

6.19:3.1 in the event that the assignee is found by the franchisee [3%] of the sale price of the Business (including any lease premium and fixtures and fittings) or

6.19:3.2 in the event that the assignee is found by the Franchisor [5%] of such sale price

6.20 Headings

Headings contained in these Conditions are for reference purposes only and shall not be incorporated in the Agreement or these Conditions and shall not be deemed to be any indication of the meaning of the clauses and sub-clauses to which they relate

6.21 Proper law

English law only shall apply to this Agreement in every particular (including formation) and the English Courts shall have sole jurisdiction to which the parties exclusively submit

APPENDIX 2

Kall-Kwik Printing (UK) Ltd
Franchise Agreement
Reproduced by kind permission of
Kall-Kwik (UK) Ltd

Franchisor: **Kall-Kwik Printing (UK) Limited**

Franchisee: ....

Address: ....

....

....

Location: ....

....

(or such other premises replacing the same in accordance with Clause 2 hereof).

Centre Number: ....

Franchise Fee: .... thousand pounds (£ ....) (not including VAT).

Date of Agreement: ....

Commencement/Opening Date: ....

The Mark:	The legend - "KALL-KWIK PRINTING" and "KALL-KWIK PRINT COPY and DESIGN" and the logos associated with the name and any additional or substitute marks which the Franchisor shall deem suitable during the Term.
The Know-How	The operational systems and methods of the Franchisor derived from Kwik-Kopy Corporation of Houston, Texas, U.S.A. and divulged to the Franchisee from time to time during the Term.
The Permitted Name:	The permitted business name of the Franchisee shall be KALL-KWIK PRINTING CENTRE NUMBER .... or such substitute permitted business name as the Franchisor shall deem suitable during the Term.
The Business:	To commence and undertake the business of instant print copying and ancillary services in the style and manner stipulated by the franchisor using the Mark and the Know-How under the Permitted Name.

The Operations Manual:	The written system of and regulations for the operation of the Business issued and amended by the Franchisor from time to time during the Term incorporating the Know-How.
The Term:	From the Commencement/ Opening Date until 8th October 2008 or sooner determination in accordance with the terms hereof.
The Continuing Fees:	Six per cent (6%) of gross sales of the Business.
The Promotional Contribution:	Four per cent (4%) of gross sales of the Business as a contribution to the advertising and promotional budget of the Franchisor to promote and expand the Mark for the benefit of all Franchisees of the Franchisor throughout the United Kingdom.

Signatories:

Signed for and on behalf of   ....
                                 Authorised Signatory of the
                                 Franchise Limited Company

Signed by   ....

Signed by   ....

Signed for and on behalf of
KALL-KWIK PRINTING
(UK) LIMITED   ....
                 Authorised Signatory

WHEREAS (1) The Franchisor warrants that it is authorised by the beneficial owner of the Mark and Know-How to enter into this Agreement.

(2) The Franchisor operates through its franchise outlets (hereinafter called "the Trade Name") a business of Instant Print and Copying Shops according to a plan or system (hereinafter called "the Method") comprising the use of the Mark Trade Name and other insignia including trade marks logos designs and other identifying materials methods of advertising and publicity, patents know-how trade secrets and the style and character of furnishings and fittings and appliances and standard operational procedures set out in the Operations Manual protected by the law of copyright or by the registration of trade marks or designs or by patent or otherwise.

(3) The Franchisee wishes to obtain a Franchise from the Franchisor for the right to use the Permitted Name and the

134

Know-How to operate the Business including all those matters referred to in Recital 2 above and to obtain the continuing assistance of the Franchisor in the on-going running of the Business and the Franchisor is willing to grant such a Franchise to the Franchisee on the terms and conditions as set out in this Agreement.

THIS AGREEMENT WITNESSETH as follows:

1.00 Grant of Franchise

1.01 Franchise Grant. IN CONSIDERATION of the Franchise Fee paid by the Franchisee to the Franchisor (receipt of which is hereby acknowledged) and in consideration of the mutual agreements covenants and undertakings herein contained the Franchisor hereby grants a Franchise to the Franchisee the right to operate the Business at the Location (the "Centre" which expression shall mean where the context so requires either or both of the Business and Location) with the right to use in connection therewith the Mark the Know-How and the Permitted Name during the Term.

1.02 Trade Mark Use. The Franchisor reserves the absolute and express right to control all uses of the Mark by the Franchisee for all purposes: The Franchisee is not permitted to use the Mark or any derivation of the same in the corporate name (if any) of the Franchisee or other legal entity except the Permitted Name during the Term shall be the sole trading name used by the Franchisee and during the Term shall not be varied in any way without the prior written consent of the Franchisor.

2.00 LOCATION OF KALL-KWIK CENTRE

2.01 Approval of Location of Centre. The Franchisor approves the site of the Centre as an acceptable site for a Kall-Kwik Centre.

2.02 Relocation of Centre. If during the Term relocation of the Centre is deemed mutually desirable by the Franchisor and the Franchisee or is required as a result of the expiration or other termination of the lease, the Franchisor will select a new location for the Centre which shall be reasonably acceptable to the Franchisee. The Franchisor shall not be responsible for any expenses or losses of the Franchisee as a result of or incidental to or arising out of any relocation of the Centre.

2.03 Lease of Premises for the Centre. If the Franchisor takes a lease or assignment of a lease of the premises for the Centre the Franchisee shall execute an Underlease in the Franchisor's standard form which will provide inter alia that default by the Franchisee under such Underlease or the termination thereof or default under this Agreement or the termination hereof shall entitle the Franchisor at its discretion to terminate the other document. If the Franchisee shall take a lease or an assignment of a lease or any other legal estate in the premises for the Centre in the Franchisee's own name then the Franchisee shall enter into a Deed of Option in the Franchisor's standard form granting the Franchisor the first right to take at Market Value (to be determined in accordance with the provision set out in Clause 11 below) the premises for the Centre, in the event that the Franchisee wishes to assign or sublet them, merge surrender or share or part with possession or occupation or otherwise transfer or dispose of the legal interest in any way to any assignee, sub-lessee, licensee or other occupier who will not be using the Centre for the Business. Any lease renewals or new lease obtained during the Term whether of the original premises for the Centre or new premises

obtained in accordance with this Clause shall be subject to the terms of this sub-clause.

2.04 The Franchisee must obtain the written approval of the Franchisor to the terms and conditions of any lease to be granted or assigned to the Franchisee.

3.00 OBLIGATIONS OF FRANCHISOR

3.01 Training at the Cost of the Franchisee. To provide training in the conduct of the Business for the Franchisee (or in the case of a corporate Franchisee one of its directors) and one initial employee at a time and place to be chosen by the Franchisor provided that Clause 4.10 below (Non-disclosure) has been complied with.

3.02 Eligibility for Training. Only a Franchisee of the Franchisor or an employee of a Franchisee shall be eligible to receive training under the terms of this Agreement.

3.03 Time of Training. Initial training will be made available to the Franchisee after execution of this Agreement. Training shall be completed within ninety (90) days of the date of this Agreement.

3.04 Training of Additional Persons. If the Franchisee requires additional training for himself or requires additional training for any employees at any mutually agreeable time after the initial training such training shall be made available by the Franchisor at the cost of the Franchisee.

3.05 Equipment. The Franchisor will arrange the supply of the initial equipment package and advise and assist the Franchisee in the requisition of all materials stock and equipment necessary for the Centre, the Franchisee being liable and responsible for the costs of all materials stock and equipment.

3.06 Decor. The Franchisor will provide the Franchisee with the designs of and advice for the fitting and decoration of the Centre and installation of equipment in the Centre. The Franchisee must obtain the prior written approval of the Franchisor to any alterations additions and conversions.

3.07 Marketing. The Franchisor will undertake a marketing and promotional programme for the Mark in the United Kingdom by such methods as it considers appropriate using the Promotional Contribution provided for below.

3.08 Expenditure. Upon written request the Franchisor will submit to the Franchisee an account of the total expenditure on advertising marketing and promotional matters in each of the Franchisor's financial years throughout the Term. In the event that the Franchisor expends sums on marketing and promotional matters in excess of the total of the Promotional Contribution from all its franchisees in any year the Franchisor shall be entitled to recoup from the total of the Promotional Contribution of all such Franchisees in any subsequent years the amount of any such excess.

3.09 Manuals. The Franchisor will issue to the Franchisee such Manuals for equipment supplies sales service advertising marketing promotion and such other matters related to the Business as the Franchisor deems appropriate, and ownership of any Manuals shall remain in the Franchisor and no right of reproduction in any form whatsoever of such Manuals is granted to the Franchisee.

3.10 Continuing Advice. The Franchisor will provide the Franchisee with continuing advice and consultation concerning the conduct of the Business throughout the Term as the Franchisor considers reasonable.

135

3.11 Records. The Franchisor will provide the Franchisee with sales reports and accounts forms to assist the Franchisee in maintaining accurate financial records.

3.12 Franchise Services Directory. The Franchisor will use best endeavours to provide all those services as set out in the Franchise Services Directory.

4.00 OBLIGATIONS OF FRANCHISEE.

The Franchisee covenants with the Franchisor as follows:

4.01 Training. Not to commence in the Business until the Franchisee (or in the case of a corporate Franchisee one director of the Franchisee) and one senior employee have received training from and have been approved as competent by the Franchisor.

4.02 Training of Personnel. To provide such training for his personnel as may be necessary to meet the qualification levels set by the Franchisor from time to time.

4.03 Attendance. To devote his full time energies and attention to the Business (and in the case of a corporate Franchisee to ensure that at least one director complies with the attention provisions of this Clause) and to procure the greatest volume of turnover for the Centre consistent with good service to his customers and the standards quality and methods stipulated in the Operations Manual.

4.04 Reports. To make such reports and keep such records concerning the Centre as the Franchisor shall from time to time require and to use all forms designated by the Franchisor, to complete and process such forms in a manner satisfactory to the Franchisor and to forward all records and forms to the Franchisor at such times and in such manner as the Franchisor from time to time require and if requested to supply to the Franchisor copies of all bank statements relating to the Business, copies of VAT returns, and till rolls.

4.05 Payment of Fees. To pay punctually any and all sums or amounts due to the Franchisor (or any other persons company body or authority) under this Agreement or under any document connected with the Franchise hereby created.

4.06 Payment of Debts and Performance of Obligations Guaranteed by the Franchisor. To pay punctually any and all sums or amounts owing by the Franchisee the payment of which has been guaranteed in any manner by the Franchisor and to perform duly and punctually any and all obligations of the Franchisee the performance of which has been guaranteed in any manner by the Franchisor.

4.07 Payment of Trade Accounts. To pay promptly all suppliers of the Franchisee and the Franchisee shall notify the Franchisor immediately of the Franchisee's inability to honour any such obligations.

4.08 Payment of Rent and Compliance with Lease. To pay promptly the rent and other payments due under the lease for the Centre such payments become due, time being of the essence. The Franchisee will not breach or default in the performance in any terms or conditions of such lease.

4.09 Trade Secrets. To keep confidential the Know-How or any other systems or methods used in the Business as divulged to the Franchisee by the Franchisor and not to reveal to any employee of the Franchisee any such information except that which is necessary for the proper conduct of the duties of the employee in the Business and to keep all such information in a secure place at the Centre accessible only to the Franchisee (or its directors in the case of a corporate Franchisee).

4.10 Non-disclosure. Not to employ any person in the Business until such person has signed a non-disclosure undertaking in the form approved by the Franchisor from time to time.

4.11 Insurance. To keep in force a comprehensive employer's and public liability policy approved by the Franchisor in respect of the Centre together with all risks insurance for the full replacement value of all equipment and stock of the Centre and loss of profits which shall include provision for the payment of the Continuing Fees and Promotional Contribution in the event of the cessation of the Business for a period of twelve months and furnish the Francnisor with a copy of such policy and in each year of the Term to supply to the Franchisor a premium payment certificate if so required by the Franchisor PROVIDED THAT if the Franchisee fails to comply with this sub-Clause the Franchisor may obtain such insurance and keep the same in force and effect and the Franchisee shall pay to the Franchisor on demand all premiums and other costs and expenses incurred by the Franchisor.

4.12 Notification to the Public. To display a notice in a prominent position at the Location clearly indicating that the Franchisee is operating an independent business under licence from the Franchisor and is not a partner agent or employee of the Franchisor.

4.13 Promote Goodwill. Constantly to protect and promote the goodwill attached to the Mark and to hold any additional goodwill generated by the Franchisee for the Mark or Permitted Name as bare trustee for the Franchisor.

4.14 Special Promotions. To co-operate with the Franchisor and other Franchisees of the Franchisor in any advertising campaign sales promotion programme or other special activity in which the Franchisor may engage or specify including the display of services advertising and the distribution of special novelties promotional literature and the like.

4.15 Conduct. To conduct himself and to ensure that his employees conduct themselves in such a manner as not to discredit or denigrate the reputation of the Business or the Permitted Name. Any behaviour amounting (in the opinion of the Franchisor) to misconduct if not promptly abated shall be a cause for termination of the Franchise in accordance with Clause 8.01 hereof.

4.16 Compliance. To use best endeavours to comply with the systems and methods as set out in the Operations Manual, Marketing Manuals and any other Manuals relating to the Operation of the Business issued by the Franchisor from time to time.

4.17 Access. To permit the Franchisor or its agents full free and unrestricted access and right of entry to the Centre for any purpose whatsoever under or pursuant to this Agreement including but not limited to checking ensuring or enforcing compliance by the Franchisee with any of his obligations hereunder whether during the Term or after his expiration or sooner determination.

4.18 Staff Standards. The Franchisee shall keep the Centre staffed with sufficient number of competent employees so as to enable the Franchisee to operate the Centre efficiently in accordance with the highest trade standards and in accordance with the standards from time to time prescribed by the Franchisor and if reasonably required by the Franchisor, to arrange staff to undergo training specified by the Franchisor.

4.19 Premises. To take possession of the Centre and open for business immediately the Centre is ready to open and to keep the Centre open for business during normal business hours or otherwise as prescribed from time to time by the Franchisor.

4.20 To keep the premises in a good state of internal repairs and decoration and to keep the premises clean and tidy and up to the reasonable demands and requirements of the Franchisor and to keep the premises internally lit and all illuminated signs lit until at least midnight of every day.

5.00 OPERATION OF KALL-KWIK CENTRE

5.01 **Business Name of Franchisee.** The business name of the Franchisee shall be the Permitted Name and no other name.

5.02 **Independent Contractor and Business.**

5.02.1 The Franchisee is and shall in all events be an independent contractor and nothing herein contained shall be construed as constituting the Franchisee as agent partner employee or representative of the Franchisor for any purpose whatsoever.

5.02.2 The Franchisee acknowledges that there is no authority granted to him under this Agreement or otherwise to incur any obligations liabilities or responsibilities on behalf of the Franchisor or to bind the Franchisor by any representations or warranties or otherwise howsoever, and the Franchisee agrees not to lead anyone to believe that the Franchisee has such authority.

5.03 **Infringement Indemnity.** To indemnify the Franchisor from any alleged unauthorised use of any patent trade mark or copyright (other than the Mark) by the Franchisee or any claim by any third party in respect of the Business or the conduct or neglect of the Franchisee or any infringement of any relevant regulations.

5.04 **Prices.** The Franchisee is free to establish prices for goods or services offered in the course of the Business at the Franchisee's sole discretion but having regard always to the Franchisor's price estimating methods and commercial viability.

5.05 **No Unsuitable Display.** The Franchisee shall ensure that the Mark is not used or displayed on any materials or products which are illegal pornographic or offensive or are critical or derogatory of any nation government religion religious body whether or not the same are associated with the Mark nor associate the Mark or the Business in any way with any political or religious movement or beliefs nor to print or distribute any materials which would denigrate the goodwill of the Mark.

5.06 **No Other Business.** Not without prior written approval of the Franchisor to permit any other business venture to operate or trade at the Centre nor without such approval to extend the scope or range of the Business at the Centre and if the Franchisor approves any such sharing or extension to procure that the gross sales of the same shall be subject to this Agreement and to pay the Continuing Fees and Promotional Contribution.

5.07 **Audit.** The Franchisee grants to the Franchisor the right at all reasonable times for the Franchisor or authorized representative to enter the Centre to make an examination and/or audit of all of the Franchisee's financial books and records including those records referred to in Clause 4.04 hereof (together with a right to make copies thereof) which can be made either by an employee of the Franchisor or by an independent contractor employed by the Franchisor for such purpose such examination and/or audit to be at the Franchisor's sole expense except as

provided below. Should the Franchisee fail to make a Sales Report to the Franchisor within thirty (30) days from the date when such Sales Report becomes due the Franchisor may examine and/or audit the Centre to determine Gross Sales and any Continuing Fees or other fees due and may charge the expenses of such examination and/or audit to the Franchisee. Furthermore should any examination and/or audit by the Franchisor of the Centre establish the Franchisee's failure to report sales or pay any royalty or fees by at least 1% of that which should have been reported or paid the Franchisor may charge the Franchisee the expense of the examination and/or audit in addition to all other payments or charges which may be due.

5.08 **Credit Sales.** Extension of credit is the sole responsibility and risk of the Franchisee and the Continuing Fees and Promotion Contribution shall be due and payable on credit sale to the same extent as if such business had been by cash sale.

6.00 FRANCHISE FEES

6.01 **Initial Payment.** The Franchisee shall pay to the Franchisor upon execution of this Agreement the Franchise Fee.

6.02 **Further Payments.** The Franchisee shall during the Term make payments to the Franchisor as follows:

6.02.1 **Dates.** To pay the Continuing Fees and the Promotional Contribution without deduction or set-off to the Franchisor or as it directs once every week every Tuesday in respect of the Business during the immediately preceding week, except that the Franchisor may waive this condition from time to time and direct and grant permission to the Franchisee to make payments monthly on or before the seventh day of each calendar month during the Term in respect of the Business during the immediately preceding calendar month, time being strictly of the essence in respect of either weekly or monthly payments.

6.02.2 **Calculations.** The Continuing Fees and the Promotional Contribution shall be calculated on the gross sales of the Centre during each calendar month or week of the Term (and for any period less than a complete calendar month or week) and gross sales shall include:

(i) all credit sales of whatever nature whether or not the Franchisee has received payment of the outstanding accounts by the Payment Date relevant to the period when such credit sales were made.

(ii) all cash sales made but not invoiced by the Franchisee in such period.

(iii) all goods sold or delivered and services performed by the Franchisee during such period which are unpaid and not invoiced on the relevant Payment Date.

(iv) all goods sold services performed and business dealings whatsoever (other than purchases) made or conducted on or from the Centre but shall exclude any Value Added Tax or any other tax or duty replacing the same during the Term.

6.02.3 **Tax Contingency.** Whenever applicable to pay to the Franchisor Valued Added Tax or any tax or duty replacing the same during the Term charged or calculated on the amount of the Franchise Fee the Continuing Fees and Promotional Contribution.

6.03 **Gross Sales Report.** On each of the Payment Dates to furnish the Franchisor with complete and accurate statements in the form approved by the Franchisor of the gross sales of the Centre since the last Payment Date and if the

Franchisee shall fail to supply the Gross Sales Report within thirty (30) days of the Payment Date the Franchisor may estimate the gross sales of the Centre by taking an average of the last six monthly figures supplied by the Franchisee. If the Franchisor makes such an estimate it will notify the Franchisee in writing of the amount of such estimate and the amount the Continuing Fees and Promotional Contribution shall upon receipt of such notice become immediately due and payable in such estimated figure. When the true amount of the gross sales is known the Franchisee will immediately pay to the Franchisor any balance outstanding together with interest thereon or in the event that the estimated figure is greater than the true figure the Franchisor will forthwith credit the Franchisee's account with the amount of any such excess but no interest shall be due and payable to the Franchisee in any event.

6.04 **Interest.** All sums due to the Franchisor under this Agreement which are not paid on the due date (without prejudice to the rights of the Franchisor and the condition that the Continuing Fees and the Promotional Contribution are paid time being of the essence) shall bear interest from day to day at the annual rate of 6% above the current Barclays Bank PLC daily interest base rate with a minimum of 12% per annum.

6.05 The Franchisee shall have trading accounts and records audited once a year during the Term and by a qualified auditor and submit a certified copy of the whole of such audited accounts to the Franchisor within three months of the end of each such year.

7.00 ASSIGNMENT AND TRANSFER.

7.01 **Assignment by Franchisor.** The Franchisor may assign charge or otherwise deal with this Agreement in any way and its rights hereunder shall inure to the benefit of its successors and assigns PROVIDED THAT any such successors and assigns shall agree in writing to assume all the Franchisor's obligations hereunder and PROVIDED FURTHER THAT any such assignment shall be made in good faith by the Franchisor. Such assignment shall discharge the Franchisor from any further obligations hereunder.

7.02.1 The Franchise hereby granted is personal and is granted to the individual Franchisee named in the particulars. Under no circumstances may the Franchisee grant a subfranchise. The Franchisee may transfer his interest in the Franchise and sell his interest in the Centre to another individual, partnership or limited company provided that the Franchisee and prospective transferee make prior written application to the Franchisor and receive written approval from the Franchisor for such transfer. The Franchisor will not unreasonably withhold its approval to such transfer provided that the transferee agrees to enter into the Franchisor's standard form of Franchise Agreement at the time in force such transfer is effected, and establishes to the satisfaction of the Franchisor that he is a respectable and responsible person with the personal capacity and financial ability to perform the obligations of a franchisee under the Franchise Agreement. Furthermore it shall be a condition of any such approval to transfer that the prospective transferee at his own cost shall satisfactorily take and complete the training then required by the Franchisor of all new franchisees prior to the prospective transferee commencing the Business. The Franchisee shall pay to the Franchisor a reasonable transfer fee to be determined by the Franchisor to cover all costs and expenses of and incidental to such transfer. Any such transfer by the Fran-

chisee under this sub-clause shall be considered a termination in respect of the Franchise for the purpose of Clause 8.0 hereof.

7.02.2 **Death of Sole Franchisee.** On the death of a sole Franchisee his personal representatives shall have six calendar months from the date of such death to notify the Franchisor of their decision:

(i) to continue the Business whereupon such personal representatives shall be deemed to be proposed assignees of the Business and the conditions set out in Clause 7.02.1 shall apply.

(ii) to assign the Business to any of the heirs of the Franchisee or to a third party whereupon the conditions set out in Clause 7.02.1 shall apply.

(iii) to terminate the Franchise Agreement and discontinue the running of the Business provided always that the personal representatives comply with the provisions and procedures set out in Clauses 9.02, 9.03, 9.04, 9.05, 9.06 below.

7.02.3 **Death of Joint Franchisee.** On the death of one of several Franchisees the survivor or survivors shall succeed in all respects to the rights of the deceased Franchisee under this Agreement.

7.02.4 **Sales Agent.** At the request of the Franchisee or his personal representatives as the case may be the Franchisor may act as a non-exclusive sales agent for the sale of the Business and in such event shall be paid a reasonable fee and its expenses for the same.

7.03 **Incorporation.** The Franchisee shall be free to incorporate and thereafter carry on the Business through any limited company owned by the Franchisee provided that the written permission of the Franchisor is first obtained and the limited company executes all agreements then required by the Franchisor for a corporate Franchisee. The Franchisee shall remain jointly and severally liable with the limited company in respect of all obligations on the part of the Franchisee contained in this Agreement and shall continue personally to supervise the Centre. Any such limited company shall be subject to all the restrictions on transferability herein contained together with a restriction on the dealing in, or sale of, or transfer or charge of the shares in the said limited company without the prior written approval of the Franchisor. A note of this restriction shall be lodged with the Register of shares and shareholding. The Franchisor shall have the right to inspect the Statutory Books of the said limited company. The Franchisee shall not be entitled to use the Permitted Name or any derivation thereof in its corporate name.

7.04 In the event that the Franchisee is in breach of the above Clause 7.03 by trading at the Centre by or through a limited company without having first obtained the written permission of the Franchisor pursuant to the provisions of Clause 7.03, this breach shall in no way affect the Franchisor's right to hold the limited company jointly and severally liable with the Franchisee and jointly and severally responsible for all the obligations and conditions referred to in this Agreement. Any such action by the Franchisor shall be entirely without prejudice and in no way affect or waive the aforementioned breach by the Franchisee of Clause 7.03 and shall not affect the Franchisor's rights in respect of that breach.

7.05 **Ownership of Corporation.** Prior to incorporation or any transfer of the Franchise to a limited company the names and addresses of the proposed shareholders and directors together with the amount and percentages of the issued share capital owned or to be owned by each shall be submitted to the Franchisor in writing and the Franchisor shall have the absolute right to accept or reject the presence of any such shareholder or director before any such transfer is made. Consideration given by the Franchisor to the acceptance of the proposed corporate Franchisee shall be the same as that given to any other new Franchisee. All directors appointed from time to time shall be required to agree in writing to be bound by the Franchise Agreement as if they were parties thereto.

7.06 **Change in Corporate Ownership.** As (in the case of a corporate Franchisee) this Franchise has been granted to the Franchisee by the Franchisor in reliance upon the quality of the directors and shareholders of the Franchisee the Franchisee will not permit any transfer or other dealing with its shares nor any change in its directors without the prior written approval of the Franchisor which shall not be unreasonably withheld in the circumstances set out in Clause 7.02.1.

7.07 **Invalid Transfer.** No transfer or assignment of the Franchisee's interest in the Franchise or the Centre shall be effective until approved in writing by the Franchisor and until the transferee has executed all agreements required by the Franchisor.

8.00 TERMINATION BY FRANCHISOR.

8.01 **For Cause.** The Franchisor shall have the right in its absolute discretion to terminate this Agreement for cause (which shall include but not be limited to a breach by the Franchisee of any obligation covenant or duty contained herein and which shall include any breach of covenants conditions and stipulations in any Lease or Underlease of the Centre) by giving written notice to the Franchisee not less than thirty (30) days prior to the date of termination and stating the reason for termination. Any such notice shall state whether the cause for termination may be remedied and if so what corrective measures are acceptable to the Franchisor.

8.02 **Correctable Cause.** If the notice of termination states that the cause for termination may be remedied then the Franchisee shall have the right to remedy the same in a manner acceptable to the Franchisor within thirty (30) days following the date of the notice and if all such causes are remedied to the satisfaction of the Franchisor within thirty (30) days then the Franchisor shall withdraw such notice.

8.03 **Repeated Cause for Termination.** Commencing with a second notice of termination for a correctable cause the Franchisor may notify the Franchisee because of a repeated cause for termination that a subsequent repeat of a given cause in the following twelve (12) month period shall be sufficient cause for a final termination which shall not be remediable.

8.04 **Insolvency.** If the Franchisee enters into liquidation or bankruptcy or suffers a receiver to be appointed or makes a composition with any creditors the Franchisor may at its sole discretion at any time thereafter terminate this Agreement on notice with immediate effect AND

8.04.1 No creditor agent employee representative or trustee of the Franchisee shall have the right to dispose of any of the equipment or materials at the Centre or to continue the Business without the prior written consent of the Franchisor.

8.04.2 Until payment of all moneys due to the Franchisor from the Franchisee on any account the Franchisor shall have a lien on any of the stock and equipment fixtures and fittings and all other items connected with the Centre not then disposed of by the Franchisee and also on any moneys received by the Franchisee in respect of the Centre.

8.05 **Low Sales Termination.** The Franchisor may at its sole discretion determine this Agreement in the event that substantial turnover arising from the Business at the Centre is not achieved within eighteen (18) months of the date of the Agreement or for a continuous period of six (6) months at any time thereafter during the Term provided that the Franchisor shall have the right (but not the duty) to appoint management personnel to supervise the Business at the expense of the Business in the event of any such failure to achieve substantial turnover to assist the Franchisee to increase sales.

8.06 **Management During Period of Notice.** At any time after the service of Notice of termination the Franchisor shall have the right (but not the duty) to appoint management personnel to supervise and manage the Premises at the expense of the Business.

8.07 **Termination of Lease Centre.** The Franchisor shall have the right in its absolute discretion to terminate this Agreement immediately upon the termination (by effluxion of time or determination for any other reason whatsoever) of the lease of the Centre unless within one (1) month following the effective date of such termination written agreement has been reached between the Franchisee and his competent Landlord within the meaning of the Landlord Tenant Act 1954 to obtain a new lease of the Centre or written agreement has been reached between the Franchisor and the new Franchisee for relocation of the Centre.

8.08 This Agreement shall be mutually terminated in the event of a transfer of the Franchise pursuant to and in accordance with Clause 7.02.1.

9.00 TERMINATION BY FRANCHISEE.

The Franchisee may terminate this Agreement at any time after the expiration of thirty-six (36) months from the commencement/opening date in the following manner:

9.01 Firstly the Franchisee confirms in writing their undertaking to continue to comply with Clause 12 of this Agreement.

9.02 Secondly serving upon the Franchisor written notice of the Franchisee's intention to surrender or assign the leasehold interest in the Centre to the Franchisor, requiring the Franchisor to give written notice of Agreement to accept such surrender or assignment of lease within two calendar months of the date of the service of such notice or alternatively requiring the Franchisor to give written notice of intention not to accept such surrender or assignment of lease within two calendar months of the date of the service of the Franchisee's notice.

9.03 In the event that the Franchisor gives written notice of agreement to accept such surrender or assignment of the lease the current edition of the then national conditions of sale shall apply to such agreement in so far as the same are not varied by the terms herein contained.

9.04 Thirdly and upon receipt of the Franchisor's Notice the Franchisee may not give less than six (6) calendar months prior written notice referred to in Clause 9.02 above to the Franchisor to terminate this Agreement.

9.05 In the event that the Franchisor serves notice agreeing to accept surrender or assignment of leasehold interest the provisions as set out in Clause 11 below shall apply. In the event that the Franchisor's notice states their intention not to accept surrender or assignment of the Franchisee's leasehold interest in the Centre the Fran-

139

chisee shall be free to assign the leasehold interest to a third party PROVIDED THAT such assignment will contain an express prohibition against use of the Centre by a third party in any business competitive with the Business or the Mark or the Business of the Franchisor for a period of five years from the date of such assignment.

9.06 The date of the legal completion of the assignment or surrender to the Franchisor as referred to in Clause 9.02 above shall be the date of the expiration of the Franchisee's notice of termination.

10.00 RIGHTS AND OBLIGATIONS UPON TERMINATION.

Upon termination of this Agreement for any reason.

10.01 **Payment of Debts to Franchisor.** The Franchisee will immediately pay to the Franchisor all sums or amounts due to the Franchisor up to the date of termination.

10.02 **Payment of Business Debts.** The Franchisee will immediately pay all debts and liabilities of the Centre giving first priority to those guaranteed by the Franchisor.

10.03 **Cease Representation.** The Franchisee will immediately cease to represent himself as a Franchisee of the Franchisor and will discontinue use of the Mark and Permitted Name and cease to operate the Business.

10.04 **Franchisor's Agency.** The Franchisor may at its sole option sell as an agent of the Franchisee all or any part of the Business including tangible and intangible assets at a price agreed upon between the Franchisor and Franchisee. If no price can be agreed upon, the Franchisor shall have the discretionary right for a period of six (6) calendar months following the termination of this Agreement to operate the Business as the Franchisee's agent. If no such bona fide offer to purchase is received within such six (6) month period acceptable to the Franchisee, then the Franchisor may thereafter liquidate the Business and apply the proceeds firstly to pay all of its reasonable costs and expenses as agent for the Franchisee secondly to satisfy the creditors of the Franchisee and then to pay over any balance remaining to the Franchisee.

10.05 **Telephone/Telex/Fax.** The Franchisee shall use his best endeavours to procure a transfer of the telephone telex and Fax number(s) of the Centre to such person as the Franchisor directs and shall indemnify the Franchisor against any cost or claim arising from such transfer.

10.06 **Premises.** The Franchisee shall deliver up and surrender possession of the Centre to the Franchisor on the termination date and do everything the Franchisor or other lessor of the Centre may require to enable the Centre to be used by the Franchisor (in such manner as it thinks fit) or by any other person nominated by the Franchisor. Notwithstanding anything herein contained it is understood and agreed that in the event of the expiration or termination of this Agreement at any time for any reason, the Franchisee shall continue to be responsible for any and all payments connected with the lease to which the Centre is subject and the Franchisee hereby indemnifies the Franchisor against any and all claims with respect thereto up to and including the date of such surrender transfer or assignment and in connection with such surrender transfer or assignment.

10.07 **Stationery and other material relating to the Centre.** The Franchisee shall destroy all stationery used in the Business and return to the Franchisor all publicity promotional and marketing material issued by the

Franchisor to the Franchisee or printed by the Franchisee and to return to the Franchisor the Operations Manual, Marketing Manuals and any other Manuals provided by the Franchisor from time to time in good condition and without having made any copies of the same and not to divulge to any third party any information concerning the Centre or the Know-How or any other systems or methods of the Franchisor used in the Business.

10.08 **Set-off.** Notwithstanding anything herein contained or implied the Franchisor shall not be obliged to pay or account to the Franchisee for any money which would otherwise be payable or owing by it to the Franchisee under or pursuant to this Agreement unless and until the Franchisee has paid satisfied or discharged all moneys debts or liabilities due or owing to the Franchisor and has satisfied all his other obligations to the Franchisor and the Franchisee hereby irrevocably authorises the Franchisor to deduct from any moneys otherwise payable by the Franchisor to the Franchisee hereunder or pursuant to this Agreement any moneys or the amount of any debts or liabilities due or owing or to become due or owing by the Franchisee to the Franchisor and to retain any moneys or amounts so deducted for its own absolute benefit.

11.00 ASSIGNMENT OR SURRENDER OF LEASEHOLD INTEREST UPON TERMINATION

11.01 In the event of the termination of this Agreement by either Franchisee or Franchisor the Franchisee shall execute and deliver such documents that may be necessary to assign to the Franchisor the benefit of the Franchisee's leasehold interest in the Centre and any fixtures and fittings therein required by the Franchisor.

11.02 If the Franchisee fails or refuses to execute such Deeds of Surrender, Assignment or other documents the Franchisor by or through any duly authorised officer or agent of the Franchisor shall have the right for and on behalf of the Franchisee to execute such Deed of Surrender, Assignment or other document. The Franchisee hereby grants to the Franchisor irrevocable right power and authority to execute on the Franchisee's behalf and in his name instead such Deeds and Documents as may be necessary in order to effect such an Assignment Surrender or Transfer.

11.03 The Franchisor shall pay to the Franchisee in consideration of such Assignment Surrender or Transfer an amount equal to market value of such leasehold interest (excluding the value of any goodwill appertaining thereto) together with the market value of any fixtures and fittings as aforesaid. Such market value shall be determined either by an agreement between Franchisor and Franchisee or failing which within 28 days after the date of such Assignment Surrender or Transfer at the joint expense of Franchisor and Franchisee by a valuer to be mutually agreed by the Franchisor and Franchisee or in default of agreement to be nominated on the application of either party by the President for the time being of the Royal Institution of Chartered Surveyors such valuer whether agreed or nominated as aforesaid shall act as an expert and not as an arbitrator and shall afford to each party an opportunity to make representrations to him and his decision shall be binding on both.

11.04 The Franchisor shall within 30 days of such determination of the valuation referred to in Clause 11.03 above as aforesaid pay to the Franchisee the amount of such market value together with such interest thereon at 3% over Barclays Bank PLC base rate from time to time prevailing from the date of such Assignment Surrender or Transfer to the date of payment subject however to the right of the Franchisor to set-off any sums due under this Agreement to the Franchisor.

11.05 The edition of National Conditions of Sale current at the date of such Assignment Surrender or Transfer shall apply to the Franchisor's right hereunder so far as the same are not varied by or inconsistent with the terms of this Agreement.

12.00 RESTRICTIONS ON FRANCHISE

12.01 **No Competition**. Without Prejudice to Clause 5.05 hereof during the Term and for a period of eighteen months after termination of this Agreement

12.01.1 not to engage directly or indirectly (whether as a director shareholder partner proprietor employee official agent or otherwise) in any business competitive with the Business or the Mark or the business of the Franchisor at the Centre

(*12.01.2 and 12.01.3 to be agreed, completed and intialled by the Parties*)

12.01.2 not to engage directly or indirectly (whether as a director shareholder partner proprietor employee official agent or otherwise) in any business competitive with the Business or the Mark or the business of the Franchisor within a .... metre radius of any Kall-Kwik Centre

12.01.3 not to engage directly or indirectly (whether as a director shareholder partner proprietor employee official agent or otherwise) in any business competitive with the Business or the Mark or the business of the Franchisor at or within a .... metre radius of the Centre.

12.01.4 At any time after termination of this Agreement not to interfere with solicit or entice any of the customers or former customers of the Business or customers of any Franchisee of the Franchisor with the intent that any of them cease to patronise the Business or the business of the Franchisor or any business of a franchisee of the Franchisor or direct their custom elsewhere.

12.02 **Confidential Information.** Except for the purposes of this Agreement during the Term and at any time thereafter the Franchisee will not disclose use or make copies of or reproduce in any form whatsoever the Operations Manual or any other Manuals issued to the Franchisee by the Franchisor or other confidential information including but not limited to confidential information concerning pricing methodology and structures advertising marketing sales promotions accounting systems business methods or procedures equipment or product studies evaluations or maintenance systems of operation and all other copyright material

13.00 MISCELLANEOUS CLAUSES

13.01 **Grant Back.** The Franchisor and Franchisee will notify each other of any improvements in the methods systems or equipment described in the Operations Manual or employed in the Business free of charge and the Franchisee shall permit the Franchisor to incorporate any such improvements notified by the Franchisee in the Operations Manual for the benefit of the Franchisor and all of its Franchisees.

13.02 **Headings.** All headings contained in this Agreement are for reference purposes only and shall not affect in any way the meaning or interpretation of this Agreement.

13.03 **Proper Law.** English Law shall apply to this Agreement and the English Courts shall have sole jurisdiction.

13.05 **Notices.** Any notice to be served on either party by the other shall be sent by pre-paid recorded delivery or registered post to the respective addresses as stated above and shall be deemed to have been received the day after posting and each party shall notify the other of any change of address within forty-eight hours of such change.

13.06 **Severance.** If any provision of this Agreement or any part thereof is declared invalid by any tribunal or court of competent jurisdiction such declaration shall not affect the validity of this Agreement and the remainder of this Agreement shall remain in full force and effect according to the terms of the remaining provisions or parts of provisions hereof.

13.07 **Force Majeure.** Both parties shall be released from their respective obligations in the event of national emergency war prohibitive governmental regulations or if any other cause beyond the control of the parties shall render the performance of this Agreement impossible whereupon

13.07.1 all the Continuing Fees and the Promotional Contribution due shall be paid immediately

13.07.2 the Franchisee shall forthwith cease the Business PROVIDED THAT this clause shall only have effect at the discretion of the Franchisor except when such event renders performance impossible for a continuous period of twelve (12) calendar months.

13.08 **Prior Obligations.** The expiration of termination of the Agreement shall not relieve either party of their respective obligations prior thereto to impair or prejudice their respective rights against the other.

13.09 **Receipt.** The receipt of moneys by the Franchisor shall not prevent either party questioning the correctness of any statement in respect of those moneys.

13.10 **Other Licences.** The Franchisor may grant a licence to any entity in the United Kingdom to manufacture any product for use in connection with the Business or displaying the Mark or for any other purposes without liability to the Franchisee.

13.11 **Other Franchisees.** The Franchisor may grant such other rights licences or franchises to any other entity in respect of the Mark in the British Isles as it decides without any liability to the Franchisee.

13.12 **Terminology.** All terms and words used in this Agreement regardless of the number and gender in which they are used shall be deemed and construed to include any other singular or plural and any other gender masculine feminine or neuter as the context or sense of this Agreement or any section paragraph or clause herein may require as if such words had been fully and properly written in the appropriate number or gender and words importing persons shall include companies and vice versa.

13.13 **Cumulative Rights and Remedies.** All rights and remedies herein conferred upon or reserved to the parties shall be cumulative and concurrent and shall be in addition to every other right or remedy given to the parties herein or at law or in equity or by statute and are not intended to be exclusive of any other right or remedy. The termination or expiration of this Agreement shall not deprive either party of any of its rights or remedies against the other.

13.14 **Joint and Several Liability.** Any covenant undertaking or agreement given or entered into by two or more persons shall be deemed to have been given or entered into by them jointly and by each of them severally so as to bind them jointly and each of them severally and each of their legal personal representative successors and assigns.

141

14.00 **Entire Agreement.**

14.01 This Agreement contains all the terms and conditions agreed upon by the parties hereto with reference to the subject matter hereof. No other Agreements oral or otherwise, shall be deemed to exist or to bind any of the parties hereto, and all prior agreements and understandings are superseded. No officer or employee or agent of the Franchisor has any authority to make any presentation undertaking warranty agreement or promise either oral or in writing not contained in this Agreement and the Franchisee agrees that he has executed this Agreement without reliance upon any such. This Agreement shall not be binding upon the Franchisor until executed by an authorised officer thereof (as distinct from any employee or sales representative thereof). This Agreement cannot be modified or changed except by written instrument signed by all of the parties hereto.

14.02 **Financial Information.** All or any financial information relating to the operation of the Franchise including but without prejudice to the generality of the foregoing forecasts budgets and performance ratios cash flow projections provided to the Franchisee by or on behalf of the Franchisor or any employee or agent of the Franchisor whether before the signing hereof or during the continuation of this Agreement shall be provided in good faith that such information is for the guidance only of the Franchisee and in no way shall be treated by the Franchisee as a warranty representation or guarantee. The Franchisee hereby acknowledges that such financial information is not to be relied upon by him without first obtaining his own independent verification thereof.

14.03 The Franchisor acknowledges that in giving advice to the Franchisee in establishing his business whether before the signing of or during the continuance of this Agreement including but without prejudice to the generality of the foregoing any financial advice, market research advice, site selection advice, recommended equipment and materials, and the assessment of the suitability of the Franchisee, the Franchisor is basing its advice and recommendation on experience actually obtained in practice and is not giving any guarantees representations or warranties beyond the expression of the view that its advice and guidance are based upon its previous experience in its dealings with its Franchisees. The Franchisee acknowledges that he has been advised by the Franchisor and that he must decide on the basis of his own judgement of what he has been told by the Franchisor or such other Franchisees whether or not to enter into this Agreement.

14.04 The Franchisee acknowledges that no representations warranties inducements guarantees or promises made by the Franchisor or representatives of the Franchisor have been relied upon save such as may have been notified by the Franchisor in writing annexed to this Agreement

14.05 **Survival of Liability.** The covenants and agreements herein which are intended by their nature to survive the cancellation termination or expiry of this Agreement shall continue in force following such cancellation termination or expiry for however long as may be required to give effect thereto.

142

Glossary

advertising levy/fee May also be called promotional levy/fee, marketing levy/fee. An identified charge on the franchisee by the franchisor, over and above the management fee, the purpose being to promote the business on a national or regional basis. The combined funds of all the franchisees make a greater impact than any single outlet could achieve. It is usual for such a fee to be identified separately in the franchise agreement, a separate fund set up, and a guarantee given that the monies will be spent on the specified activity with provision for an audit and independent examination of the fund by the franchisees.

advisory council Sometimes called franchisee association or review council. The name given to a representative body of franchisees within a specific franchise nominated by the franchisor or elected by the franchisees. The purpose is to explore new ideas and opportunities through regular meetings with the franchisor. Usually such bodies are formed at the instigation of the franchisor but have also been formed by dissatisfied franchisees with the objective of bringing pressure to bear on the franchisor.

assignment A clause, common in franchise contracts, giving the franchisee the right to assign the agreement usually to a person approved by the franchisor.

bank franchisee finance package In 1981 Barclays and NatWest banks appointed franchise managers, since emulated by all the major high street banks. Working primarily with franchisors these managers and their staff examine franchise opportunities and will often offer a funding scheme enabling the prospective franchisee to purchase the franchise. Up to 70 per cent of the total cost of the franchise may be available. These schemes are effected through the branch network and may be a combination of facilities including term loans, overdrafts and delayed terms for capital and/or interest repayments.

blueprint A term used in franchising to describe the format (as in business format) or plan developed by the franchisor to describe the complete system for the successful operation of the business.

British Franchise Association (BFA) The franchisor's trade association founded in 1977 by eight of the early UK franchising companies with the objective of raising the profile of ethical franchising in the UK.

business-format franchise   A franchise term where the franchisor provides a complete formula, blueprint, plan or format for operating the total business, where the franchisor is actively involved in establishing the franchisee's business both initially and ongoing, and the franchisee can build equity in the business.

company-owned units/outlets   *See also* pilot operations. Outlets owned, operated and managed by the franchisor, they may be used for training as well as a testbed for new ideas and programmes. They can, more simply, be a continuing source of income to the franchisor. The overwhelming majority of McDonald's restaurants in the UK are company owned.

competition laws   Competition laws applicable in the UK are the Fair Trading Act 1973, the Restrictive Trade Practices Act 1976, and, in the EEC, the Treaty of Rome, Article 85, dealing with competition, and Article 86, dealing with monopoly situations. The purpose of competition law is to increase competition between companies or organizations through the removal of restraints on trade or monopoly situations. The clauses in franchise contracts most likely to cause problems with competition laws are full-line forcing, tied-in-sales and restricted or exclusive areas.

continuing fee   *See* franchise fee.

contract – franchise contract   The agreement between the franchisor and the franchisee describing the terms of the agreement, the rights and obligations of both parties.

disenfranchise   The withdrawal of the rights of the franchise, whether it be a franchise to vote or to operate a business format business system.

ethical franchise   A franchise that is operated according to ethical business standards usually referring to the ethics as promulgated by the British Franchise Association.

European Franchise Federation (EFF)   The EFF comprises the National Franchise Trade Associations in different European countries which includes the British Franchise Association. It is located in Brussels at this point in time.

exclusive area   A territory assigned to a franchisee with undertakings that the franchisor will not trade in the area nor will other franchisees be appointed or allowed to trade within the area. There is a difficulty in giving total exclusivity within the Restrictive Trade Practices Act 1976.

fast-food franchise   Food outlets usually offering a limited menu, served quickly. Encompasses counter service, table service and take-away outlets. Wimpy and Kentucky Fried Chicken were the first in the UK, McDonald's is the largest, currently opening a new store somewhere in the world every 15 hours.

first-generation franchise   Usually used to identify early franchises – car manufacturers, oil companies and soft drink bottlers who used franchising principally as a means of distribution.

fixed fee   *See* franchise fee.

fractional franchise   Where the franchise is only a part of the franchisee's interest. Usually related to premises, a franchise shop within department stores is a good example.

franchise fee   There are two types of franchise fee common in franchising: the initial fee and the ongoing fee. The initial fee, sometimes called the front-end fee, is a one-off payment designed to cover the costs of the franchisor in recruiting and setting up the franchisee. The ongoing service fee, sometimes referred to as royalties or management fees and most commonly based on a percentage of sales turnover, is the usual way for the franchisor to obtain his continuing income from the franchisee. Occasionally a franchisor will choose to charge a fixed fee on a weekly or monthly basis.

franchisee   The individual, company or partnership which buys a franchise or licence from the franchisor. Variously referred to as licensee, franchise owner or associate.

franchisee association/advisory council   *See* advisory council.

franchisor   The company which operates the franchise and sells franchises to franchisees. In some cases the franchisor can be a franchisee of a franchisor himself, in other words an intermediary franchisee – *see* master licensee.

front-end fee   *See* franchise fee.

International Franchise Association (IFA)   The United States of America, USA Franchise Trade Association.

investment franchise   'Investment', 'job' and 'business' franchises are terms coined in an attempt to classify franchising. An 'investment' franchise is more expensive than the others but has never been quantified.

job franchise   A term coined in an attempt to categorize franchising along with investment and business. A 'job' franchise is usually described as low-level investment where the franchisee works in the business.

joint venture A method whereby a franchisor, usually from overseas, will seek to establish a legal relationship with a partner in a foreign market and share the costs of getting up a franchise organization. Commonly the franchisor initiating the idea will contribute the know-how and expect the host country partner to provide the funds and management.

know-how The intellectual property – the systems, methods and expertise of the franchisor. Usually referred to as know-how in the contract.

licensee *See* franchisee.

licensing agreement *See* franchise agreement.

location franchise A franchise operating from fixed premises where the premises tend to be an important part of the business operation, i.e. retail premises where customers visit.

management service fee *See* franchise fee.

mark The name by which the franchisor's business is known and which the franchisee will be permitted to use.

marketing levy *See* advertising levy.

master licensee A franchisee who usually has responsibility for more than one outlet and is commonly totally responsible for the development of the franchised business (through other franchisees) in an area. As an example, the UK arm of ServiceMaster was originally a master licensee in Europe.

mobile franchise Usually a vehicle operated franchise which goes out to serve customers, e.g. windscreen replacement, car tuning and cleaning services. The opposite to a location franchise.

monthly fee *See* franchise fee.

multiple franchise Commonly refers to a franchisee who operates more than one, of a specific franchise, outlet.

network Usually used to describe the whole franchise organization. Could be a UK network or world-wide network.

non-exclusive area Theoretically the opposite of exclusive areas but usually qualified to assure the franchisee of some protection.

operations manuals Now a generic term used to describe all the manuals provided by a franchisor to a franchisee to operate the business. These will include administrative as well as actual operational manuals.

pilot unit The term used to describe the test model or outlet set up by the franchisor. *See also* company-owned units/outlets.

promotional levy *See* advertising levy.

pyramid selling Pyramid selling is a marketing system, erroneously associated with franchising in the past, which involves selling distributorships through a tiered structure. The founders of such schemes rely primarily on selling distributorships rather than products. The business has been outlawed in the UK.

review council *See* advisory council.

royalties *See* franchise fee. The use of this term within a franchise may raise questions with the Inland Revenue. Traditionally royalties are paid on copyrighted works of art such as literature and music and different tax arrangements may apply.

second-generation franchises A term commonly used to describe the franchises which started in and since the franchise boom of the 1950s.

service fee *See* franchise fee.

service mark The mark registered by a service organization applied to services rather than products. A few years ago it was not possible to register service marks in the UK and the British Franchise Association and its members lobbied MPs and produced a turn-around in Government thinking on this.

sub-franchises A term used to describe franchisees set up by an existing franchisee, usually a master franchisee.

territorial rights The rights granted by the franchisor to the franchisee within the area allocated. Franchisees will usually seek some understanding that they will not be in competition with other franchisees or the franchisor within their territory.

turnkey operation Basically an expression for a business format franchise where the franchisee turns the key in the door with the business ready to run.

up-front fee *See* franchise fee, initial fee.

Barclays Guides for the Small Business

The following titles are available in this series:

Wilson: *Financial Management for the Small Business* 0 631 17254 8
Rogers: *Marketing for the Small Business* 0 631 17247 5
Aziz: *Computing for the Small Business* 0 631 17256 4
Wilson: *International Trade for the Small Business* 0 631 17252 1
Maitland: *Managing Staff for the Small Business* 0 631 17482 6
Lloyd: *Law for the Small Business* 0 631 17349 8
Stanworth & Smith: *Franchising for the Small Business* 0 631 17498 2
Gray: *Managing Growth in the Small Business* 0 631 17249 1
Gammon: *Buying and Selling for the Small Business* 0 631 17528 8
All titles are £6.95 each.

You can order through your local bookseller or, in case of difficulty, direct from the publisher using this order form. Please indicate the quantity of books you require in the boxes above and complete the details form below. The publisher will be pleased to negotiate a discount for orders of more than 20 copies of one title.

Payment
Please add £2.50 to payment to cover p&p.

☐ Please charge my Mastercard/Visa/American Express account

card number ☐☐☐☐☐☐☐☐☐☐☐☐☐☐☐☐☐

Expiry date _____

Signature _____
(credit card orders must be signed to be valid)

☐ I enclose a cheque for £_____ made payable to **Marston Book Services Ltd**
(PLEASE PRINT)

Name _____

Address _____

_____

_____ Postcode _____

Tel No _____

Signature _____ Date _____

Please return the completed form with remittance to:
Department DM, Basil Blackwell Ltd
108 Cowley Road, Oxford OX4 1JF, UK
or telephone your credit card order on 0865 791155.

Goods will be despatched within 14 days of receipt of order. Data supplied may be used to inform you about other Basil Blackwell publications in relevant fields.
Registered in England No. 180277 Basil Blackwell Ltd.

Printed and bound by CPI Group (UK) Ltd, Croydon, CR0 4YY

16/04/2025

14658825-0001